What readers are saying about
Pragmatic Version Control using Subversion

I expected a lot, but you surprised me with even more. Having used CVS for years I hesitated to try Subversion until now, although I knew it would solve many of the shortcomings of CVS. After reading your book, my excuses to stay with CVS disappeared. Oh, and coming from the Pragmatic Bookshelf this book is fun to read too. Thanks Mike.

> ► **Steffen Gemkow**
> Managing Director, ObjectFab GmbH

I'm a long-time user of CVS and I've been skeptical of Subversion, wondering if it would ever be "ready for prime time." Until now. Thanks to Mike Mason for writing a clear, concise, gentle introduction to this new tool. After reading this book, I'm actually excited about the possibilities for version control that Subversion brings to the table.

> ► **David Rupp**
> Senior Software Engineer, Great-West Life & Annuity

This was exactly the Subversion book I was waiting for. As a long-time Perforce and CVS user and administrator, and in my role as an agile tools coach, I wanted a compact book that told me just what I needed to know. This is it.

Within a couple of hours I was up and running against remote Subversion servers, and setting up my own local servers too. Mike uses a lot of command-line examples to guide the reader, and as a Windows user I was worried at first. My fears were unfounded though—Mike's examples were so clear that I think I'll stick to using the command line from now on! I thoroughly recommend this book to anyone getting started using or administering Subversion.

> ► **Mike Roberts**
> Project co-Lead, CruiseControl.NET

Pragmatic Version Control

using Subversion

Pragmatic Version Control

using Subversion

Mike Mason

The Pragmatic Bookshelf

Raleigh, North Carolina   Dallas, Texas

Many of the designations used by manufacturers and sellers to distinguish their products are claimed as trademarks. Where those designations appear in this book, and The Pragmatic Programmers, LLC was aware of a trademark claim, the designations have been printed in initial capital letters or in all capitals. The Pragmatic Starter Kit, The Pragmatic Programmer, Pragmatic Programming, Pragmatic Bookshelf and the linking *g* device are trademarks of The Pragmatic Programmers, LLC.

Every precaution was taken in the preparation of this book. However, the publisher assumes no responsibility for errors or omissions, or for damages that may result from the use of information (including program listings) contained herein.

Our Pragmatic courses, workshops, and other products can help you and your team create better software and have more fun. For more information, as well as the latest Pragmatic titles, please visit us at

```
http://www.pragmaticprogrammer.com
```

ISBN 0-9745140-6-3

Printed on acid-free paper with 85% recycled, 30% post-consumer content.

First printing, February 2005

Version: 2005-1-14

Contents

Preface

I was pretty excited when I heard about the Pragmatic Starter Kit—finally some guidance on the basic stuff all projects need to get right. The opportunity to produce a Subversion edition of *Pragmatic Version Control* was one I couldn't miss. Subversion had previously saved me (and my team) from version control hell, and I wanted to do my part to help promote a great new version control system.

Version control adds an immense amount to a project. It gives you a safety net, helps your team collaborate effectively, lets you organize your builds and QA, and even allows you to do some detective work if things go wrong. I hope this new edition of *Pragmatic Version Control* will help you and your team get started and succeed with Subversion.

Acknowledgments

I'd like to thank Dave and Andy for taking a chance on me being able to write the book and to thank Dave being such an excellent editor. I wasn't really sure what I was getting myself into, and Dave's advice and guidance were invaluable.

The book received plenty of scrutiny by reviewers; I'd like to thank Brad Appleton, Branko Čibej, Martin Fowler, Steffen Gemkow, Robert Rasmussen, Mike Roberts, and David Rupp for their well-thought-out comments and suggestions. I'm frankly amazed by the quality of feedback I got—great suggestions, highly technical comments and plenty of people thinking about the "bigger picture."

Everyone at ThoughtWorks has been really supportive of my book writing efforts, including several people who took the time to look through early drafts of the book, and I'd like to thank all those who gave me advice and guidance. I'd particularly like to thank the Calgary office for welcoming me into the fold this year and for enabling me to get stuff finished when the crunch point came.

Finally I'd like to thank Martin, Mike, and Michelle for making me believe I could really write the book and for their encouragement along the way.

Mike Mason
December 2004
`mike@mikemason.ca`

Typographic Conventions

italic font   Italics indicate a term that is being defined, or borrowed from another language.

files   Files (and directories) are indicated like this.

commands   Commands (and options such as -h) are shown like this.

output   Output (as well as things you might need to type) is indicated like this. If commands are too long for a single line they're split onto multiple lines using a \ (backward slash).

CVS Hint: This kind of text indicates a hint for users familiar with CVS.

This warning sign indicates this material is more advanced and can be skipped on your first reading.

"Joe the developer," our cartoon friend, asks a related question that you may find useful.

Chapter 1

Introduction

This book tells you how to improve the effectiveness of your software development process using version control.

Version control, sometimes called *source code control*, is the first leg of our project support tripod. We view the use of version control as mandatory on all projects.

Version control offers many advantages to both teams and individuals:

- It gives the team a project-wide undo button; nothing is final, and mistakes are easily rolled back. Imagine you're using the world's most sophisticated word processor. It has every function imaginable, except one. For some reason, they forgot to add support for a DELETE key. Think how carefully and slowly you'd have to type, particularly as you got near the end of a large document. One mistake, and you'd have to start again. It's the same with version control; having the ability to go back an hour, a day, or a week frees your team to work quickly, confident that they have a way of fixing mistakes.

- It allows multiple developers to work on the same code base in a controlled manner. The team no longer loses changes when someone overwrites the edits made by another team member.

- The version control system keeps a record of the changes made over time. If you come across some "surprising code," it's easy to find out who made the change, when, and (with any luck) why.

- A version control system allows you to support multiple releases of your software at the same time as you continue with the main line of development. With a version control system, there's no longer a need for the team to stop work during a code freeze just before release.

- Version control is a project-wide time machine, allowing you to dial in a date and see exactly what the project looked like on that date. This is useful for research, but it is essential for regenerating prior releases for customers with problems.

This book focuses on version control from a project perspective. Rather than simply listing the commands available in a version control system, we explain the tasks you need to perform well in a successful project and then show how a version control system can help.

Let's start with a small story....

1.1 Version Control in Action

Fred rolls into the office eager to continue working on the new Orinoco book ordering system. (Why Orinoco? Fred's company uses the names of rivers for all internal projects.) After getting his first cup of coffee, Fred updates his local copy of the project's source code with the latest versions from the central version control system. In the log that lists the updated files, he notices that Wilma has changed code in the basic Orders class. Fred gets worried that this change might affect his work, but today Wilma is off at the client's site, installing the latest release, so he can't ask her directly. Instead, Fred asks the version control system to display the notes associated with the change to Orders. Wilma's comment does little to reassure him:

```
Added new deliveryPreferences field to the Orders class
```

To find out what's going on, he goes back to the version control system and asks to see the actual changes made to the source file. He sees that Wilma has added a couple of instance variables, but they are set to default values, and nothing seems to change them. This might be a problem in the future, but it is nothing that will stop him today, so Fred continues working.

As he works on his code, Fred adds a new class and a couple of test classes to the system. Fred adds the names of the files he creates to the version control system as he creates them; the files themselves won't be added until he commits his changes, but adding their names now means he won't forget to add them later.

A couple of hours into the day, Fred has completed the first part of some new functionality. It passes its tests, and it won't affect anything in the rest of the system, so he decides to check it all into the version control system, making it available to the rest of the team. Over the years, Fred has found that checking code in and out frequently works best for him: it's a lot easier to reconcile the occasional conflict if you have to worry about only a couple of files rather than a week's worth of changes from the whole team.

Why You Should Never Answer the Phone

Just as Fred is about to start the next round of coding, his phone rings. It's Wilma, calling from the client's site. It looks like there's a bug in the release she is installing: printed invoices are not calculating sales tax on shipping amounts. The client is going ballistic, and they need a fix now.

...Unless You Use Version Control

Fred double-checks the name of the release with Wilma and then tells the version control system to check out all the files in that version of the software. He puts it in a temporary directory on his PC, as he intends to delete it after he finishes the work. He now has two copies of the system's source code on his computer: the trunk (the main line of development) and the version released to the client. Because he is about to fix a bug, he tells the version control system to tag his source code with a label. (He'll add another tag when he has fixed the bug. These tags act as flags you leave behind to mark significant points in the development. By using consistently named tags before and after he makes the change, other folks in his team will be able to see exactly what changed should they look at it later.)

In order to isolate the problem, Fred first writes a test. Sure enough, it looks like no one ever checked the sales tax calculation when shipping was involved, because his test immediately shows the problem. (Fred makes a note to raise this during this iteration's review meeting; this is something that should never have gone out the door.) Sighing, Fred adds the line of code that adds shipping to the taxable total, compiles, and checks that his test passes. He reruns the whole test suite as a quick sanity test and checks the fixed code back into the central version control system. Finally, he tags the release branch indicating that the bug is fixed. He sends a note off to QA, who is responsible for shipping emergency releases to the client. Using his tag, they'll be able to instruct the build system to produce a delivery disk that includes his fix. Fred then phones Wilma and tells her the fix is in the hands of QA and should be with her soon.

Having finished with this little distraction, Fred removes the source for the released code from his local machine: there's no point in cluttering things up, and the changes he has made are safely tucked back into the central server. He then gets to wondering: is the sales tax bug he found in the released code also present in the current development version? The quickest way to check is to add the test he wrote in the released version to the development test suite. He tells the version control system to merge that particular change in the release branch into the appropriate file in the development copy. The merge process takes whatever changes were made to the release files and makes the same changes to the development version. When he runs the tests, his new test fails: the bug is indeed present. He then moves his fix from the release branch into the development version. (He doesn't need the release branch's code on his machine to do any of this; all the changes are being fetched from the central version control system.) Once he has the tests all running again, he commits this change into the version control system. That's one less bug that'll bite the team next time.

Crisis over, Fred gets back to working on his own tasks for the day. He spends a happy afternoon writing tests and code and toward the end of the day decides he is done. While he has been working, other folks in his team have also been making changes, so he uses the version control system to take their work and apply it his local copy of the source. He runs the tests one last time and then checks his changes back in, ready to start work the next day.

Tomorrow...

Unfortunately, the next day brings its own surprises. Overnight Fred's central heating finally gives up the ghost. As Fred lives in Minnesota, and as it's February, this isn't something to be taken lightly. Fred calls into work to say he'll be out most of the day waiting for the repair folks to arrive.

However, that doesn't mean he has to stop working. Accessing his office network using a secure connection over the public Internet, Fred checks out the latest development code onto his laptop. Because he checked in before he went home the previous night, everything is there and up-to-date. He continues to work at home, wrapped in a blanket and sitting by the fire. Before he stops for the day, he checks his changes in from the laptop so they'll be available to him at work the next day. Life is good (except for the heating repair bill).

Storybook Projects

The correct use of version control on Fred and Wilma's project was pretty unobtrusive, but it gave them control and helped them communicate, even when Wilma was miles away. Fred could research changes made to code and apply a bug fix to multiple releases of their application. Their version control system supports offline work, so Fred gained a degree of location independence: he could work from home during his heating problems. Because they had version control in place (and they knew how to use it), Fred and Wilma dealt with a number of project emergencies without experiencing the panic that so often characterizes our response to the unexpected.

Using version control gave Fred and Wilma the control and the flexibility to deal with the vagaries of the real world. That's what this book is all about.

1.2 Road Map

Chapter 2 introduces the concepts and terminology of version control systems. Many version control systems are available from which to choose. In this book we're going to focus on Subversion, an open-source tool available for free over the internet. Subversion is the successor to CVS, which is itself one of the most popular version control systems available.

Chapter 3, *Getting Started with Subversion*, is a tutorial introduction to using Subversion. The remainder of the book is a set of recipes for using Subversion in projects, divided into six main chapters. Each chapter contains a number of recipes:

- Connecting to Subversion in different ways

- Using common Subversion commands

- Organizing files inside Subversion

- Using tags and branches to handle releases and experimental code

- Creating a project

- Handling third-party code

We end with a set of appendixes providing reference information and more in-depth discussion on using Subversion:

- Networking, securing, and backing up your repository

- Migrating to Subversion

- Using Third-party Subversion tools

- Summary of recipes and Subversion commands

- Using other resources available on the Internet

1.3 Why Choose Subversion

Whilst this book is about version control in general, we're choosing to focus on Subversion as our tool of choice. Since a significant number of different version control tools are available, it's probably worth mentioning why you'd want to pick Subversion.

The Subversion project was started by a team of developers who had extensive experience with CVS (some of them had literally written books on the subject) but who had decided the time had come to replace the aging system. The Subversion developers were painfully aware of CVS's shortcomings and made sure they designed a high-performance, modern version control system. Their goal was not to create a radical new paradigm in version control—the CVS development model had proven highly successful—but to replace CVS with a new system that fixed all of CVS's wrinkles.

This might not sound like Subversion is anything groundbreaking, but bear in mind that CVS is already miles ahead of many other version control tools. Subversion's feature set puts it at the forefront of what's available today.

Versioning for Files, Directories, and Metadata

Directories, as well as files, are versionable objects in Subversion. This means that moving or renaming a directory is a first-class operation—files within the directory automatically move with it, and history is preserved correctly.

Files and directories can also have metadata associated with them using Subversion properties. Properties can be textual or binary and are versioned in the same way as file contents, changing over time, being merged with newer revisions, etc. Properties are used extensively to control how Subversion handles files, keyword expansion, stuff you'd like it to ignore, and so on. The great thing about properties is that any Subversion client can access them, allowing third-party tools to integrate much more elegantly with your repository.

Atomic Commits and Changesets

Subversion uses a database transaction analogy when a user commits a change to the repository, making sure that either the entire change is successfully committed or it's aborted and rolled back. It's also impossible to see half a change whilst someone is making a commit—you'll see the state of the repository either before the change or after. This behavior is known as *atomic commit* and is useful because every developer will always have a consistent view of the repository. If your network connection goes down whilst you're committing a change, you won't leave half your changes in the repository, and the change will be rolled back cleanly.

revision

revision number

As part of the atomic commit process, Subversion groups all of your changes into a *revision* (sometimes called a *changeset*) and assigns a *revision number* to the change. By grouping changes to multiple files into a single logical unit, developers are able to better organize and track their changes.

Excellent Networking Support

Subversion has a highly efficient network protocol and stores pristine copies of your working files locally, allowing a user to see what changes they've made without even contacting the server. Subversion provides a variety of networking options, including the ability to leverage Secure Shell (SSH) and the Apache web server to make repositories available over a public network.

Cheap Branching, Tagging, and Merging

In many version control systems, creating a branch is a big deal. In CVS, for example, branching or labeling code requires the server to access and modify every file in the repository! Subversion uses an efficient database model to branch and merge files, making these operations quick and painless.

True Cross-Platform Support

Subversion is available for a wide variety of platforms, and, most important, the server will run well on Windows. This significantly lowers the barrier to entry for teams that don't have a Unix server available and makes it much easier to get started—you can set up a server on a spare Windows box (or even one that's in use!) and migrate to another machine once Subversion has proven itself.

## Chapter 2

What Is Version Control?

A version control system is a place to store all the various revisions of the stuff you write while developing an application. They're basically very simple. Unfortunately, over the years, people have started using different terms for the various components of version control. And this can lead to confusion. So let's start by defining some of the terms *we'll* be using.

2.1 The Repository

You may have noticed that we wimped out; we said that "a version control system is a place to store...the stuff you write," but we never said exactly where all this stuff is stored. In fact, it all goes in the *repository*.

repository

In almost all version control systems, the repository is a central place that holds the master copy of all versions of your project's files. Some version control systems use a database as the repository, some use regular files, and some use a combination of the two. Either way, the repository is clearly a pivotal component of your version control strategy. You need it sitting on a safe, secure, and reliable machine. And it should go without saying that it needs to get backed up regularly.

In the old days, the repository and all its users had to share a machine (or at least share a filesystem). This turns out to be fairly limiting; it was hard to have developers working at different sites or working on different kinds of machines or operating systems. As a result, most version control systems today support networked operation; as a developer you can

---

Different Flavors of Networked Access

The writers of version control systems sometimes have different definitions of what *networked* means. For some, it means accessing the files in a repository over shared network drives (such as Windows shares or NFS mounts). For others it means having a client-server architecture, where clients interact with server repositories over a network. Both can work (although the former is hard to design correctly if the underlying file-sharing mechanism doesn't support locking reliably). However, you may find that deployment and security issues dictate which systems you can use.

If a version control system needs access to shared drives, and you need to access it from outside your internal network, then you'll need to make sure your organization allows you to access the data this way. Virtual Private Network (VPN) packages allow this kind of secure access, but not all companies run VPNs.

Subversion uses the client-server model for remote access.

---

access the repository over a network, with the repository acting as a server and the version control tools acting as clients. This is tremendously enabling. It doesn't matter where the developers are; as long as they can connect over a network to the repository, they can access all the project's code and its history. And they can do it securely; you can even use the Internet to access your repository without sharing your precious source code with a nosy competitor.

This does lead to an interesting question, though. What happens if you need to do development but you don't have a network connection to your repository? The simple answer is, "it depends." Some version control systems are designed solely for use while connected to the repository; it is assumed that you'll always be online and that you won't be able to change source code without first contacting the central repository. Other systems are more lenient. The Subversion system, which we use for our examples in this book, is one of the latter. We can edit away on our laptops at 35,000 feet and then resynchronize the changes when we get to our hotel rooms. This online/offline issue is a crucial one when choosing a version control system; make sure that whatever product you choose supports your style of working.

Some version control systems support the notion of multiple repositories instead of a single central repository. Developers can swap sets of changes between the separate repositories. These are often called *decentralized* version control systems and are popular when large numbers of developers need to operate semiautonomously, most famously for developing the Linux kernel. Examples of decentralized version control systems include BitKeeper, Arch, and SVK. These systems have a very different style of development, and we won't discuss them further in this book.

2.2 What Should We Store?

All the things in your project are stored in the repository. But what exactly are the *things* we're talking about?

Well, you obviously need program source files to build your project: the Java, C#, Ruby, or whatever language you're using to write your application. In fact, some folks think that this source code is such an important component of version control that they use the term *source code control systems*.

The source code is certainly important, but many people make the mistake of forgetting all the other things that need to be stored under version control. For example, if you're a Java programmer, you may use the Ant tool to compile your source. Ant uses a script, normally called build.xml, to control what it does. This script is part of the build process; without it you can't build the application, so it should be stored in the version control system.

Similarly, many projects use metadata to drive their configuration. This metadata should be in the repository too. So should any scripts you use to create a release CD, test data used by QA, and so on.

In fact, there's an easy test when it comes to deciding what goes in and what stays out. Simply ask yourself "if we didn't have an up-to-date version of x, could we build, test, and deliver our application?" If the answer is "no," then x should be in the repository.

As well as all the files that go toward creating the released software, you should also store your noncode project artifacts under version control (anything you'll need to make sense of things later), including the project's documentation (both internal and external). It might also include the text of significant e-mails, minutes of meetings, information you find on the web—anything that contributes to the project.

2.3 Working Copies and Manipulating Files

The repository stores all the files in our project, but that doesn't help us much if we need to add some magic new feature into our application; we need the files where *we* can get to them. This place is called our local *working copy*.

working copy

The working copy is a local copy of all of the things that we need from the repository to work on our part of the project. For small- to medium-sized projects, the working copy will probably simply be a copy of all the code and other artifacts in the project. For larger projects, you may arrange things so that developers can work with just a subset of the project's code, saving them time when building and helping to isolate subsystems of the system. You might also hear the working copy called the *working directory* or simply the *workspace*.

In order to populate our working copy initially, we need to get things out of the repository. Different version control systems have different names for this process, but the most common (and the one used by Subversion) is *checking out*. When you check out from the repository, you extract local copies of files into your working copy. Even if you do your work on the same computer that stores the repository, you'll still need to check files out before using them; the repository should be treated as a black box. The checkout process ensures that you get up-to-date copies of the files you request and that these files are copied into a directory structure that mirrors that of the repository.

checking out

Joe Asks...
What about Generated Artifacts?

If we store all the things needed to build the project, does that mean we should also be storing all the generated files? For example, we might run JavaDoc to generate the API documentation for our source tree. Should that documentation be stored in the version control system's repository?

The simple answer is "no." If a generated file can be reconstituted from other files, then storing it is simply duplication. Why is this duplication bad? It isn't because we're worried about wasting disk space. It's because we don't want things to get out of step. If we store the source and the documentation, and then change the source, the documentation is now outdated. If we forget to update it and check it back in, we've now got misleading documentation in our repository. So in this case, we'd want to keep a single source of the information, the source code. The same rules apply to most generated artifacts.

Pragmatically, some artifacts are difficult to regenerate. For example, you may have only a single license for a tool that generates a file needed by all the developers, or a particular artifact may take hours to create. In these cases, it makes sense to store the generated artifacts in the repository. The developer with the tool's license can create the file, or a fast machine somewhere can create the expensive artifact. These can be checked in, and all other developers can then work from these generated files.

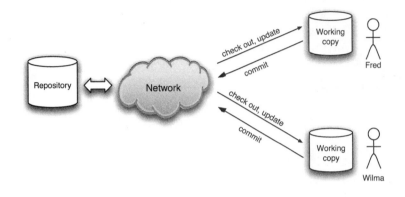

Figure 2.1: The Repository and Working Copies

---

export

It's also possible to *export* files from the repository, which is slightly different from checking out. When you do an export, you won't end up with a working copy; you'll just get a snapshot of files from the repository. This is useful in certain situations such as packaging code for distribution.

As you work on a project, you'll make changes to the project's code in your working copy. Every now and then you'll reach a point where you'll want to save your changes back to the repository. This process is called *committing* your changes back into the repository.

committing

Of course, all the time you're making changes, so are other members of your team. Just like you, they'll be committing their changes to the repository. However, these changes do not affect your local working copy; it doesn't suddenly change just because someone else saved changes into the repository. Instead, you have to instruct the version control system to *update* your working copy. During the update, you'll receive the latest set of files from the repository. And when your colleagues do an update, they'll receive your latest changes too. (Just to confuse things, however, some folks also use the term *check out* to refer to updating, because they are checking out the latest changes. Because this is a common idiom, we'll also use this at times in this book.) These various interactions are shown in Figure 2.1.

update

Of course there's a potential problem here: what happens if you and a colleague both want to make changes to the same source file at the same time? It depends on the version control system you're using, but all have ways of dealing with the situation. We talk about this more in Section 2.9, *Locking Options*, on page 23.

2.4 Projects, Directories, and Files

So far we've talked about storing *things*, but we haven't talked about how those things are organized.

At the lowest level, most version control systems deal with individual files.[1] Each file in your project is stored by name in the repository; if you add a file called Panel.java to the repository, then other members of your team can check out Panel.java into their own working copies.

However, that's pretty low-level. A typical project might have hundreds or thousands of files, and a typical company might have dozens of projects. Fortunately, almost all version control systems allow you to structure the repository. At the top level, they typically divide your work into projects. Within each project, they let you work in terms of modules (and often submodules). For example, perhaps you are working on Orinoco, a large web-based book ordering application. All the files needed to build the application might be stored in the repository under the Orinoco project name. If you wanted to, you could check it all out onto your local disk.

The Orinoco project itself might be broken down into a number of largely independent modules. For example, there might be a team working on credit card processing and another working on order fulfillment. With any luck, the folks in the credit card subproject won't need to have all the project's source to do their job; their code should be nicely partitioned. So when they check out, they really want to see only the parts of the project that they're working on.

---

[1] Some IDE-like environments perform versioning at the method level, but they're fairly uncommon.

externals

Subversion organizes the repository into directories. A project might correspond to a top-level directory, with modules and submodules arranged as directories within your project. This might be enough for simple projects, but for more complex code sharing Subversion supports the notion of *externals*. An externals definition allows you to include another Subversion repository location in any directory in your project.

CVS Hint: Subversion's directory-based organization corresponds, roughly speaking, to CVS modules, with externals corresponding to *alias modules*. Organizing stuff by directory turns out to be just as powerful and a lot easier for people to understand.

Subversion's "everything is a directory" approach is discussed in more depth in Chapter 7, *Organizing Your Repository*, on page 101.

2.5 Where Do Versions Come In?

This book is all about version control systems, but so far all we've talked about is storing and retrieving files in a repository. Where do versions come in?

Behind the scenes, a version control system's repository is a fairly clever beast. It doesn't just store the current copy of each of the files in its care. Instead it stores *every version* that has ever been checked in. If you check out a file, edit it, and then check it back in, the repository will hold both the original version and the version that contains your changes. In reality, most version control systems store the differences between versions of a file, rather than complete copies of each revision. Subversion stores the full text for the newest revision of a file, as well as cleverly picking historical revisions to store in full, so that it can retrieve any version of a file quickly. This helps minimize disk space requirements while keeping updates and checkouts fast.

There are two common numbering schemes for version control systems: *file-specific numbering* and *repository-wide numbering*. In a file-specific numbering scheme, the first revision of a file is named 1.1. When a change is checked in, the file is given the number 1.2, and so on. If you have version 1.2 of Node.cs and version 1.6 of Graph.cs, committing a change to

Node.cs will make it revision 1.3. Graph.cs remains unchanged and at revision 1.6.

In the repository-wide numbering scheme, the entire repository starts at revision 0, and checking in a change increases the repository revision number to 1, then 2, and so on. In this scheme, it's more correct to talk about "Panel.java *at* revision 7" than to talk about "revision 7 *of* Panel.java." Subversion uses this second numbering scheme, which turns out to be extremely useful for referring to changes once they've been committed. Section 8.5, *Simple Bug Fixes*, on page 115 explains how to use revision numbers for merging bug fixes across branches.

CVS Hint: CVS uses a file-specific numbering scheme, so people often look at the revision number of a file to try to gauge how much activity is occurring in the file or how much has changed over a period of time. Subversion's repository-wide revision numbers make it impossible to do the same thing—you'll have to use Subversion's log command to examine the history to look for changes.

Subversion's repository revision numbers act as a kind of marker pen, drawing a line through all the files in your repository each time a commit is made. Figure 2.2 on the following page shows three files: Trains.java, Graph.java, and Node.java. First we commit a change to Graph.java (shown in the diagram as Graph.java's circle changing to a star), taking the repository to revision 2. If we then change Trains.java and Node.java, we'll bring the repository to revision 3. The key point is that Graph.java is at revision 3 as well, even though its content has not changed since revision 2.

Subversion revision numbers aren't much use for figuring out how much has changed in a particular file or group of files,[2] so don't try to use them for that. People used to the file-specific numbering scheme are often confused that the repository has jumped a bunch of revisions without them checking in any-

---

[2]Using version numbers, no matter how they're assigned, to try to track "how much change is happening" is pretty futile—a single change could affect every line in a file. You're probably better off looking at the changes directly, using your version control system's history browsing features, if you want to find out how much has changed.

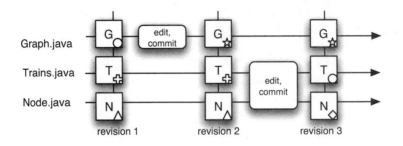

Figure 2.2: REVISION NUMBERS IN THE REPOSITORY

thing. This makes sense when you realize the number applies to everyone's checkins, not just your own.

This system of storing revisions is remarkably powerful. Using it, the version control system can do things such as

- Retrieve a specific revision of a file.

- Check out all of the source code of a system exactly as it appeared two months ago.

- Tell you what changed in a particular file between revisions 7 and 9.

You can also use the revision system to undo mistakes. If you get to the end of the week and discover you've been going down a blind alley, you can back out all the changes you've made, reverting to the code as it was on Monday morning.

2.6 Tags

All these revision numbers are great, but as people we seem to be better at remembering names such as PreRelease2 rather than numbers such as r347.

Tags

Tags to the rescue. Version control systems let you assign names to a group of files (or directories or an entire project) at a particular point in time. If you assigned the tag PreRelease2 to our group of three files, you could subsequently check them out using that same tag.

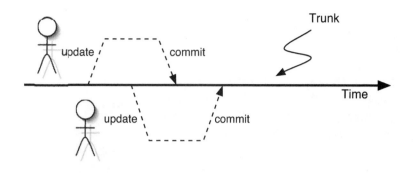

Figure 2.3: A SIMPLE TRUNK

Tags are a great way of keeping track of significant events in the life of your project's code. We'll be using tags extensively later in this book. You can read about tags and branches (the topic of the next section) in Chapter 8, *Using Tags and Branches*, on page 105.

2.7 Branches

In the normal course of development, most folks are working on a common code base (although they'll likely be working on different parts of it). Developers will be checking out code, making changes in their working copies, then checking the changes back in, and everyone will share this work. This main body of code is called the *trunk*. We show this in Figure 2.3. In this figure (and in the ones that follow) time flows from left to right. The thicker horizontal line represents the progression of code through time; it is the main line of the development. Individual developers check in and check out code from the trunk into their individual working copies. *trunk*

But consider the time when a new release is about to be shipped. One small subteam of developers may be preparing the software for that release, fixing last-minute bugs, working with the release engineers, and helping the QA team. During this vital period, they need stability; it would set back their efforts if other developers were also editing the code, adding features intended for the next release.

One option is to freeze new development while the release is being generated, but this means the rest of the team is effectively sitting idle.

Another option would be to copy the source software out onto a spare machine and then have the release team just use this machine. But if we do that, what happens to the changes they make after the copy? How do we keep track of them? If they find bugs in the release code that are also in the trunk, how can we efficiently and reliably merge these fixes back in? And once they've released the software, how do we fix bugs that customers report; how can we guarantee to find the source code in the same state as when we shipped the release?

branching

A far better option is to use the *branching* capabilities built into version control systems.

Branching is a bit like the hackneyed device in science fiction stories where some event causes time to split. From that point forward there are two parallel futures. Some other event occurs, and one of these futures splits too. Soon you're dealing with a whole bunch of alternative universes (a great device for resolving the story when you run out of plot ideas).

Branching in a version control system also allows you to create multiple parallel futures, but rather than being populated by aliens and space cowboys, they contain source code and version information.

Take the case of the team about to release a new version of the product. So far, all the team has been working in the *trunk*, the common thread of code shown in Figure 2.3 on the page before. But the release subteam wants to isolate themselves from the trunk. To do this, they create a branch in the repository. From now until their work is done, the release subteam will check out from and check into this branch. Even after the application is released, this branch will stay active; if customers report bugs, the team will fix them in this release branch. This is shown in Figure 2.4 on the facing page.

A branch is almost like having a totally separate repository: people using that branch see the source code it contains and operate independently of people working on other branches or the trunk. Each branch has its own history and tracks changes independently of the trunk (although obviously if you

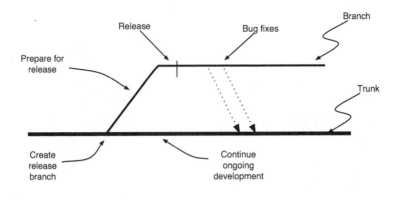

Figure 2.4: TRUNK WITH A RELEASE BRANCH

look back past the point where the branch was made you'll see that the branch and the trunk become one).

This is exactly what you want when you're creating releases. The team working on the release will have a stable code base to polish and ship. In the meantime, the main group of developers can continue making changes to the main line of code; there's no need for a code freeze while the release takes place. And when customers report problems in the release, the team will have access to the code in the release branch so they can fix the bugs and ship updated releases without including any of the newly developed code from the trunk.

Branches are stored as named directories within Subversion; you create a branch simply by copying the trunk to a new location. Subversion's internals use *lazy copies* to make this *lazy copies* copying process efficient, and these lazy copies are the basis of Subversion's tagging support too. Whenever you copy a file or directory, Subversion simply stores a link to the original. When you make a change to the copy, Subversion records those changes as differences against the original. Using lazy copies Subversion can very quickly copy large trees of files using almost zero space, ideal for branches and tags.

You can create branches off other branches, but typically you won't want to; we've come across many developers who have been put off branching for life because of some bad experiences with overly complicated branching in a project.

You should avoid excessive branching. Even though branches might seem like a cheap way to hedge your bets during development, they have significant costs when you need to merge changes between branches. Not only do you need to merge different lines of development, you have to make sure you don't lose any changes in the process. Bear in mind that the need to create multiple branches, especially for parallel lines of development rather than releases, may be a sign that something is going wrong.

In this book we'll describe a simple scheme that does everything you'll need but that avoids unnecessary complexity.

2.8 Merging

Back to the science fiction story with the multiple alternate futures. In order to spice up the plot, writers often allow their characters to travel between these different universes using wormholes, polyphase deconfabulating oscillotrons, or just a good strong cup of piping-hot tea.

You can also travel between alternate futures in a version control system (the cup of tea is optional). Although each checked-out version comes from a particular branch and gets checked back into that same branch, it's easy to have multiple branches checked out on a single developer's machine (in different directories or folders on the hard drive, of course). That way a developer can be working on both the trunk and on (say) bug fixes in a release branch at the same time.

merging

Even better, version control systems support *merging*. Say you fix a bug in the release branch and realize that the same bug will be present in the trunk code. You can tell the version control system to work out the changes you made on the release branch to fix the bug and then to apply those changes to the code in the trunk. You can even merge them into different release branches. This largely eliminates the need to cut and paste changes back and forth between different versions of a system. We'll have a lot to say about merging later.

2.9 Locking Options

Imagine two developers, Fred and Wilma, working on the same project. Each has checked out the project's files onto their respective local hard drives, and each wants to edit their local copy of File1.java. What happens when they come to check that file in?

A bad scenario would be for the version control system to accept Fred's changes and then accept Wilma's version of the same file. As Wilma's copy won't have Fred's changes in it, storing Wilma's copy in the repository will effectively forget all Fred's hard work.

To stop this happening, version control systems implement some form of conflict resolution system (probably a good thing in the case of Fred and Wilma). There are two common versions of conflict resolution.

The first is called *strict locking*. In a strict locking version control system, all files that are checked out are initially flagged as being "read-only." You can look at them, and you can use them to build your application, but you can't edit or change them. To do that, you have to ask the repository's permission: "please can I edit File1.java?" If no one else is editing that same file, then the repository gives you permission and changes the permissions of your local copy of the file to be "read/write." You can then edit. If anyone else asks to edit that same file while you have it flagged, they'll be refused. After you've finished your changes and checked the file in, your local copy reverts to being read only, and it becomes available for other folks to edit.

strict locking

The second form of conflict resolution is often called *optimistic locking*, although it really is no locking at all. Here, every developer gets to edit any checked-out file: the files are checked out in a read/write state. However, the repository will not allow you to check in a file that has been updated in the repository since you last checked it out. Instead, it asks you to update your local copy of the file to include the latest repository changes before checking in. This is where the cleverness lies. Instead of simply overwriting all your hard work with the latest repository version of the file, the version control system attempts to merge the repository changes with your changes.

optimistic locking

For example, let's look at File1.java:

```
Line 1    public class File1 {
            public String getName() {
              return "Wibble";
            }
  5         public int getSize() {
              return 42;
            }
          }
```

Wilma and Fred both check this file out. Fred changes line 3:

```
    return "WIBBLE";
```

He then checks the file in. This means that Wilma's copy of the file is out-of-date. Not knowing this, Wilma changes line 6, so it returns 99 instead of 42. When she goes to check the file in, she's told that her copy is out-of-date; she needs to merge in the repository changes. This corresponds to the star marked *OUT OF SYNC* in Figure 2.5 on the next page.

When Wilma merges the changes into her file, the version control system is clever enough to spot that Fred's changes do not overlap hers, so it simply updates her local copy with a new line 3, leaving her changes still in her file. When she checks in, she'll be storing her changes and leaving Fred's intact.

What happens if Fred and Wilma both updated line 3 but made different changes to it? Assuming Fred checks in first, his changes will be accepted. When Wilma goes to check in, she'll again be told that her copy is out-of-date. This time, though, when she goes to merge in the repository version the system will notice that she's made a change to a line that has also been changed in the repository. There's a conflict. In this case, Wilma will see some warning messages, and the conflict will be marked up in her copy of the source file. She'll have to resolve it manually (probably by talking with Fred to find out why they were both working on the same line of code).

Given this description, you might think that optimistic locking is a somewhat reckless way of developing systems: multiple people editing the same files at the same time. Often people who haven't tried it reason that it can't work and insist on working only with version control systems that implement strict locking.

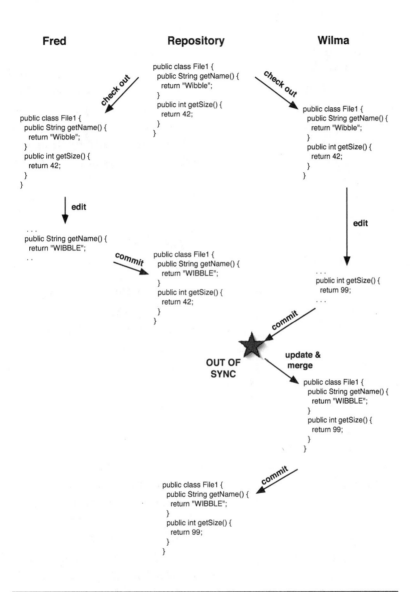

Figure 2.5: FRED AND WILMA MAKE CHANGES TO THE SAME FILE, BUT THE CONFLICT IS HANDLED BY A MERGE.

In reality, though, strict locking turns out to be a lot of extra hassle with no particular payback. If you try an optimistic locking system (such as Subversion), you'll be surprised at just how rarely conflicts arise. It turns out that in practice the normal ways of dividing work on a team mean that people work on different areas of the code; they don't bump into each other that often. And when they *do* need to edit the same file, they're often working on different parts of it. In a strict locking system, one would have to wait for the other to finish and check in before proceeding. In an optimistic locking system, both can proceed. We've tried both kinds of locking over the years, and our strong recommendation is that the vast majority of teams should use a version control system with optimistic locking.

2.10 Configuration Management (CM)

Sometimes you'll hear folks talking about Configuration Management or Software Configuration Management systems (or flinging about the abbreviations CM or SCM). At first sight they seem to be talking about version control. And that's largely true; the practices of CM rely very heavily on having good version control in place. But version control is just one tool used by configuration management.

CM is a set of project management practices that enables you to accurately and reproducibly deliver software. It uses version control to achieve its technical goals but also uses a lot of human controls and cross-checks to make sure things are not forgotten. You can think of configuration management as a way of identifying the things that get delivered and version control as a means of recording that identification. CM is a large topic, and we won't be covering it more in this book. If you're interested in CM, *Software Configuration Management Patterns* [BA03] is an excellent resource, and goes into greater detail on many of the issues we don't have room to cover in detail.

For now, though, let's concentrate on how we can use version control systems to get our jobs done. The next chapter is a gentle introduction to one particular version control system, Subversion.

Chapter 3

Getting Started with Subversion

The best way to get familiar with a new software tool is to try it, so this chapter will show you how to create and work with a live Subversion repository. You'll be learning the basic steps in using Subversion whilst maintaining a trivial project.

Since Subversion is reasonably recent software, you will probably need to install it on your computer. Basic installation, which we'll cover in this chapter, is pretty simple. For more advanced installation, networking, security, and administration instructions, see Appendix A on page 147.

Subversion ships with a command-line client, but there are a variety of third-party tools for interacting with your repository. TortoiseSVN integrates with the Windows Explorer, for example, and some IDEs now include Subversion support.

3.1 Installing Subversion

Obviously you need to have Subversion installed before you can use it. Depending on how Subversion is packaged for your operating system, you might get the option to install the client and server components separately. This is more common for Unix platforms where an adminstrator might want to set up a server without installing client tools.

 Joe Asks...

Shells, Prompts, Command Windows??

Terminology can get confusing when you're dealing with command lines, so let's clear things up a bit.

A command processor, also called a *shell*, is a program that accepts a command and executes it. The command can have parameters, and the command processor often has additional capabilities (such as redirecting the application's output to a file). Under Windows, cmd and command are common command processors (which you use depends on which version of Windows you use). On Unix boxes, there's a great choice of shells, from the original sh, through csh, bash, tcsh, zsh, and so on.

Back before we had GUI systems, the command processor or shell was how you interacted with your computer. When you booted up DOS, you got the DOS prompt, and you were talking with the command application; your computer monitor was effectively a dumb terminal.

Now that we have fancy front ends, we need a place to run these command processors, so folks have written terminal applications that run in windows. When one of these terminal applications is running a command processor or a shell, you can type in commands at the prompt and have them execute. Sometimes we'll call these windows executing a command processor a *command window*.

Figure 3.1: WINDOWS COMMAND PROMPT

Our first step is to check if Subversion is already installed on your computer. The easiest way to do this is with the command line. If you're familiar with the command line, you can skip the next section.

The Command Line

The command line is a low-level facility that lets you run commands directly on your computer. The command line is a powerful tool, but it can also be fairly cryptic: you're working down in the engine room when you're issuing commands.

On Windows boxes, you can get to a command-line window by using *Start > Run* and typing cmd as the name of the program to run (on some older Windows versions you may have to type command instead). You should see a window that looks like Figure 3.1.

On Unix boxes, you may be working at the command line already. If instead you use a desktop environment such as Gnome or KDE, look for the terminal, konsole, or xterm application and run it. You should see a window like that in Figure 3.2 on the following page. If you're using Mac OS X, your shell application is hidden in /Applications/Utilities/Terminal.

You use the command-line window to enter commands and view their output; no GUI front ends here. For example, in the

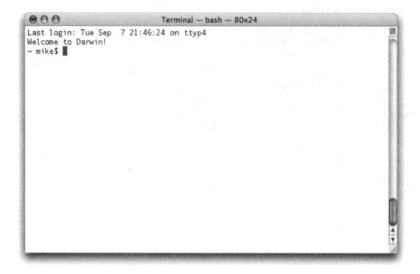

Figure 3.2: UNIX SHELL PROMPT

command-line window you just created, enter the following command and hit the Enter key (sometimes labeled Return):

```
echo Hello
```

You should see the text "Hello" echoed back at you, and just below it a new prompt where you can enter another command. An example is shown in Figure 3.3 on the next page.

Prompts

One of the joys of the command window is that you can customize the prompt that the shell uses to tell you it's ready for input. You can include the time, the current directory, your username, and all sorts of other essential information in the prompt. Unfortunately, this flexibility can also lead to confusion: looking at the previous screenshots you can see that the Windows prompt looks different from the Unix prompt.

In this book, we'll try to simplify things by standardizing on a generic prompt in our examples. We'll show the name of the current directory followed by a greater-than sign (>). For example, we might give an example of a command as follows:

```
work> svn update
```

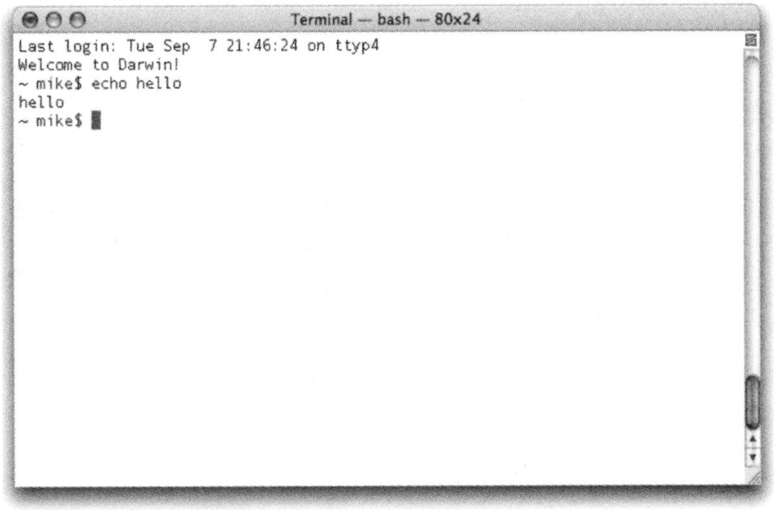

```
Last login: Tue Sep  7 21:46:24 on ttyp4
Welcome to Darwin!
~ mike$ echo hello
hello
~ mike$ 
```

Figure 3.3: AFTER ECHOING "HELLO"

This means we're in a directory called work and we issued the command svn update. It should be simple to map this "logical" prompt to the prompt you actually see in your operating system's command window.

The commands in this book are generally not Windows or Unix specific: they should work on both systems. The only differences are in the names of files; Windows uses drive letters and backward slashes between the components of filenames, and Unix uses forward slashes. Use appropriate filenames for your environment, and things should work out fine. An exception to this rule is when dealing with file://-based repositories—the Windows and Unix syntax is quite a bit different. When this is the case, we'll include both Windows and Unix versions of each command.

Checking If Subversion Is Installed

Bring up a command window on your computer, and type the command svn --version, followed by the Return key. If the Subversion client is installed correctly, you'll see a response similar to that in Figure 3.4 on the following page. Next try

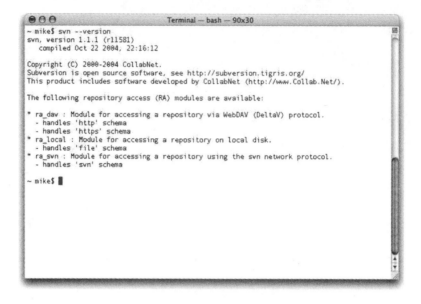

Figure 3.4: SUBVERSION CLIENT INSTALLED CORRECTLY

svnadmin --version to see if the Subversion administration tools are installed. If both of these commands worked, you can skip ahead to the next section.

Most likely your computer complained that it couldn't find svn or svnadmin. That's okay—Subversion is not yet a standard part of most operating system installs, so it was a long shot anyhow. Subversion is distributed both as source code and as binary packages for different operating systems. Complete instructions for your operating system should be available from the package download page at http://subversion.tigris.org/project_packages.html. You can also download the source code if you want to compile Subversion yourself, but since Subversion relies on a number of other packages, it may be easiest to download a precompiled version.

3.2 Creating a Repository

Subversion requires a repository to store your data. In this section you'll create a repository for storing your first project.

> **Subversion Versions**
>
> Whilst this book was being written, Subversion 1.1.2 was the latest release. All the examples in the book will work with both Subversion 1.0.x and 1.1.x, but we recommend using the newer version.

First off you need to create an empty directory for the repository and then tell Subversion to create a new repository in the directory. Let's suppose you're using /home/mike/svn-repos (for Unix) or c:\svn-repos (for Windows).

Windows:

```
mkdir c:\svn-repos
svnadmin create c:\svn-repos
```

Unix:

```
mkdir /home/mike/svn-repos
svnadmin create /home/mike/svn-repos
```

Once the svnadmin command completes, you'll end up with a set of files in your repository directory. We'll go into more detail later on how the repository is stored on disk, but for now you can safely treat the repository directory and its contents as a black box.

Your Subversion repository is now set up—next we'll start creating a project.

3.3 Creating a Simple Project

Let's populate your repository with a new project. In the spirit of pioneering Internet startups, we'll use a cryptic yet cool-sounding project name—*Sesame*. We'll start by creating a couple of files and then import them into a sesame directory in the repository. (The project name is officially Sesame, but we'll use the lowercase *sesame* in our repository.)

Create a temporary directory on your computer called tmpdir. Inside that directory, use your favourite text editor to create two files: Day.txt and Number.txt.

Using Remote Filesystems

If you're using a remote filesystem, such as a Windows home directory on a network share or your Unix home directory mounted over NFS, the Subversion client will work great. You can check out a working copy to any kind of networked drive with no problems.

If you're running the Subversion *server*, however, you must make sure the repository directory you initialize with svnadmin create is on a *local drive*.

This is basically because of the way Subversion uses Berkeley DB as the backend in which the repository is stored. BDB doesn't like using database files on a network drive because of the way it maps them into memory.

If you want to store your repository on a network drive, you need to use the "fsfs" filesystem–based backend instead of BDB, for which you'll need Subversion 1.1. Just add the `--fs-type fsfs` option when creating your repository.

File Day.txt:

```
monday
tuesday
wednesday
thursday
friday
```

File Number.txt:

```
zero
one
two
three
four
```

These don't look much like source programs, but remember that we're using our repository to store *all* the stuff we need to build our project. It looks like Sesame needs to know the names of the days of the week and a few small numbers, and these are the data files that help it do this.

We now need to tell Subversion to import these files into a new project in the repository. Subversion organizes everything in the repository by directory, which we'll explain in more detail in Chapter 7, *Organizing Your Repository*, on page 101. For now, we'll use the convention recommended by the Subversion developers and store our Sesame project in /sesame/trunk.

In your command prompt, change to the tmpdir directory. If you're on Windows, run

```
tmpdir> svn import -m "importing Sesame project"       \
          . file:///c:/svn-repos/sesame/trunk
Adding           Number.txt
Adding           Day.txt
Committed revision 1.
```

Don't type the backward slash after the log message. We ran out of space and couldn't fit the whole command on one line, so we used \ to separate it over several lines. You'll see this used quite often throughout the book.

If instead you're on Unix, run

```
tmpdir> svn import -m "importing Sesame project"       \
          . file:///home/mike/svn-repos/sesame/trunk
Adding           Number.txt
Adding           Day.txt
Committed revision 1.
```

The import keyword tells Subversion we want to import some files to our repository. The -m option allows you to associate a message with this import. It's a good idea to use a log message indicating what kind of import you've performed.

The next parameter (.) tells Subversion to import the contents of the current directory, tmpdir, into the repository.

The final parameter is a repository URL describing where we want to import the files. Here we're telling Subversion to look on the local filesystem for the repository in our svn-repos directory and to import into /sesame/trunk inside it.[1]

Subversion responds by letting us know that it has added the two files and has *committed* the change into the repository.

So, now we've got these files safely tucked away in the repository. If we are brave (or foolish), we can go ahead and delete the copies in our temporary directory. However, the prudent

---

[1]We're importing to /sesame/trunk because in future the Sesame project will need to support branches, which will be stored in /sesame/branches. This is discussed more fully in Chapter 7, *Organizing Your Repository*, on page 101.

Repository URLs

You may have noticed that when we imported our files into the repository, we used a `file://...` URL to tell Subversion where to put the new project. This syntax looks a lot like Internet addresses you see in a web browser, except instead of starting with `http://` the URL starts with `file://`. This tells Subversion to look on the local filesystem for the repository, instead of on the web.

In Chapter 5, *Accessing a Repository*, on page 55 you'll see how you can use different URLs to access a Subversion repository via a network, either on a web server or via the custom `svn` protocol.

(and pragmatic) developer would probably want to verify that they are indeed correctly stored in the repository before deleting them. And the easiest way to do that is to get Subversion to check the files in the Sesame project out into your local work area. Once we've confirmed that everything is there, and that it looks correct, we can delete our originals. The next section shows how this is done.

3.4 Starting to Work with a Project

It doesn't matter whether you're starting work with a new project (such as project Sesame, which we just created) or if you're joining a project that has been running for months and has thousands of source files. What you do to start working with the project's files is the same:

1. Decide where to put the working copies of the files on your local machine.

2. Check the project out of the repository into that location.

The first decision is normally fairly simple. We tend to have a single directory on our boxes called work. We then check out all projects somewhere under this directory. For simple projects, we tend to check out directly under work. For more complex ones, maybe involving code branches, we'd organize things into a few subdirectories. For now, let's assume we are

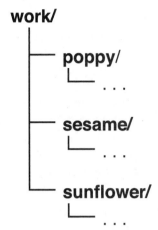

work/
- **poppy/**
  - . . .
- **sesame/**
  - . . .
- **sunflower/**
  - . . .

Figure 3.5: WORKING DIRECTORY LAYOUT

working with simple projects. If we have checked out three separate projects called poppy, sesame, and sunflower, we'd end up with directories that looked something like Figure 3.5.

So, if you haven't already got one, let's start off by creating a work directory, either from the command line or using your File Manager.

Windows: `mkdir c:\work`

Unix: `mkdir /home/mike/work`

Now we'll check out the source into our working directory. We use a `file://` URL to specify our repository, so again this command looks a little different on Windows and Unix. Change to your work directory, and then on Windows run

```
work> svn co file:///c:/svn-repos/sesame/trunk sesame
A   sesame\Number.txt
A   sesame\Day.txt
Checked out revision 1.
```

On Unix, you need to run

```
work> svn co file:///home/mike/svn-repos/sesame/trunk sesame
A   sesame/Number.txt
A   sesame/Day.txt
Checked out revision 1.
```

The argument co tells Subversion that we want to perform a checkout, the file:// URL specifies which repository we want to check out from, and finally we tell Subversion where we want to put our working copy, in this case inside a sesame directory in our working directory.

You now have a local copy of the Sesame project containing the two files that we initially imported. From now on, we'll be working with these copies of the files, because these are the ones that are being managed by Subversion. After checking that they look correct, we can go ahead and delete the original copies in our temporary directory. We've handed control of these files over to our version control system, and it's just too confusing to have the original and the managed copies lying around on our machine. We'll make sesame our current directory and work with the checked-out files.

3.5 Making Changes

Despite all our hard work, our customer comes back complaining; it appears our software needs to work at weekends. So, fire up your favorite editor and add two lines to the end of Day.txt:

```
monday
tuesday
wednesday
thursday
friday
saturday
sunday
```

After saving these changes to disk, let's see what Subversion now thinks about the state of our project. You can use the svn status command to get the status of one or more files:

```
sesame> svn status Day.txt
M       Day.txt
```

The M here is showing us that Subversion recognizes that this file has been modified locally (and that these changes have not yet been saved in the repository).

If we do all our work in small increments, it's easy to remember what changes we made to individual files. However, if you've forgotten why a file has been modified (or if you just want to double-check), you can use the svn diff command to show the changes between the repository version of the file and your local copy:

```
sesame> svn diff Day.txt
Index: Day.txt
===================================================================
--- Day.txt      (revision 1)
+++ Day.txt      (working copy)
@@ -3,3 +3,5 @@
 wednesday
 thursday
 friday
+saturday
+sunday
```

The output contains a bunch of information. The first line tells us the name of the file being examined. This has a couple of uses. First, if we're examining a bunch of files with one command, it helps us identify where we are. Second, it is also used when generating patches (but that's not something we'll be looking at for a while yet).

The two lines after the row of equals signs tell us the name and revision number of the repository file and that we're comparing it with the working copy.

The cryptic @@ -3,3 +3,5 @@ tells us where in the file the differences are, followed by the actual difference. The lines starting with + mean they've been added, and a line starting with - would mean it has been removed.

This diff is shown in *unified* format, meaning that it contains context information as well as lines that have been changed. It's a popular format because it's easy to read, and the extra context allows changes to be applied even if the original file has been altered slightly. Subversion also allows us to specify our own diff program using --diff-cmd. This is useful if we want to use a graphical diff utility, for example.

This is an area where the GUI front ends to Subversion have a distinct advantage: if you use such a tool, you should be able to generate nice color-coded displays of file differences.

3.6 Updating the Repository

Having made our changes (and of course having run the unit tests), we're ready to save our latest version in the repository.

On a single-person project such as Sesame, this is really very simple—you use the svn commit command:

```
sesame> svn commit -m "Client wants us to work on weekends"
Sending        Day.txt
Transmitting file data .
Committed revision 2.
```

The commit function is used to save any changes we've made back to the repository. The -m option is used to attach a meaningful message to the changes.

Even though we asked Subversion to commit all files in the Sesame project, it's clever enough to know that Number.txt has not changed, so only the changes in Day.txt are sent to the repository.

Subversion tells us it has "committed revision 2." It's important to note that this means revision 2 of the whole repository, not just Day.txt. If we had changed both Day.txt and Number.txt, we'd still be at revision 2 in the repository. You can think of Subversion revision numbers as kind of a global marker going all the way through the repository, recording when each set of changes went in.

Following the commit, you can use the log function to confirm that the repository has indeed been updated:

```
sesame> svn log Day.txt
------------------------------------------------------------
r2 | mike | 2004-09-08 21:54:19 -0600 (Wed, 08 Sep 2004)
Client wants us to work on weekends
------------------------------------------------------------
r1 | mike | 2004-09-08 21:50:13 -0600 (Wed, 08 Sep 2004)
importing Sesame project
------------------------------------------------------------
```

We can see that mike was the last user to change Day.txt, in revision 2 (r2) of the repository, and we can see the log message that was used when adding Saturday and Sunday to our list of days. We can also see that Day.txt was changed in revision 1, when we imported the Sesame project. If you use --verbose, Subversion will tell you exactly what changed with each revision:

```
sesame> svn log --verbose Day.txt
------------------------------------------------------------
r2 | mike | 2004-09-08 21:54:19 -0600 (Wed, 08 Sep 2004)
Changed paths:
   M /sesame/trunk/Day.txt
Client wants us to work on weekends
------------------------------------------------------------
r1 | mike | 2004-09-08 21:50:13 -0600 (Wed, 08 Sep 2004)
```

```
Changed paths:
   A /sesame
   A /sesame/trunk
   A /sesame/trunk/Day.txt
   A /sesame/trunk/Number.txt
importing Sesame project
------------------------------------------------------------
```

Now that Subversion is being extra talkative, we can see that in revision 2 /sesame/trunk/Day.txt was modified—there's an M next to it. For revision 1, we can see that the /sesame directory and contents were created. Because of the way Subversion tracks commits—changes to a set of files, all saved at once and associated with a single log message—it can display all the files that were changed in each commit, even though we asked only about Day.txt. This can be extremely useful, for example, when reviewing historical information when tracking down a bug.

Mixed Revision Working Copies

In the last example we used svn log to look at the history of Day.txt. In fact, using svn log without any other arguments produces a log for the current directory and any subdirectories, starting with the most recent changes and working backward.

If you ask for the log of the current directory immediately after committing a change to Day.txt, Subversion won't tell you about your change. This is a bit counterintuitive—after all the change is in the repository, we can see it if we ask for the log for Day.txt—so why isn't Subversion including it in the log for the current directory?

The answer is that because Subversion tracks directories as first-class objects, it remembers the revision number for each directory in your working copy. When we commit a change to Day.txt, Subversion knows the working copy is at revision 2, but the actual directory is still at revision 1. In order to see the log message, you'll need to run svn update first, updating the current directory to revision 2.

Most of the time you can just ignore mixed revisions. If you do get tripped up by this behavior, a quick svn update will fix the problem. In the recipes shown later in the book, we'll often include an update as the first step, helping to avoid this problem altogether.

Setting Up a Message Editor

Whenever you change the repository by importing files, committing changes, or copying things around, you need to enter a log message. If you don't specify the -m option, Subversion will try to open an editor for you to type in a log message.

Subversion looks at environment variables to determine which editor it should use, trying SVN_EDITOR, VISUAL, and EDITOR. If you're on Windows and would like to set your editor to Notepad, open a command prompt and type

```
work> set SVN_EDITOR=notepad
```

This will set SVN_EDITOR only for the lifetime of your command window. If you want to set the environment variable permanently, you need to go into Windows' Control Panel (switch to Classic View if you're using Windows XP) and choose System. Under the Advanced tab, hit the Environment Variables button, and create a new variable. The variable name should be SVN_EDITOR, and the value should be notepad. After setting up the new environment variable, you'll need to close any open command windows and re-open them for the new setting to take effect.

If you're a Unix user, you'll set environment variables differently depending on the shell you're using. Try looking at .profile, .bashrc, or .cshrc in your home directory for existing environment variables, and then add a new one. You may need to log out and back in again for a new setting to take effect.

3.7 When Worlds Collide

Everyone gets nervous when they first hear that Subversion doesn't lock files for editing. They wonder, "what happens if two people edit the same file at the same time?" In this section we'll find out (and hopefully in the process put to rest any worries you may have). To do this, we'll need another user (so that we can have multiple people editing a file at the same time). Unfortunately, our supplier of do-it-yourself human cloning kits is on the run, so we'll have to make do with simulating the other you.

When it comes to handling conflicts, Subversion doesn't really know about users. Instead, it cares about making sure that different working copies are consistent with the repository. This means we can simulate our second user simply by checking out a new copy of our project; we just need to put it in a different place than the first copy. When we first checked out our project, we put it in a directory called sesame, which is the project name. To check it out again, we'll need to specify a different location, a directory parallel to the one we've been working in. Let's call that directory aladdin. To check out on Windows, change to your work directory and run

```
work> svn co file:///c:/svn-repos/sesame/trunk aladdin
A   aladdin\Number.txt
A   aladdin\Day.txt
Checked out revision 2.
```

On a Unix system, you need to run

```
work> svn co file:///home/mike/svn-repos/sesame/trunk aladdin
A   aladdin/Number.txt
A   aladdin/Day.txt
Checked out revision 2.
```

We've checked out the project we've been working on all along (Sesame) from the same repository. But we tell Subversion to store the files in a new directory, called aladdin. Because we checked in the files from our original directory, we now have two copies of the project on our hard drive, one in sesame, the other in aladdin. Right now the two sets of files are identical (skeptical readers, feel free to check). Remember that two different directories are our simulation of having two people working on our project, each with their own checked-out copy of the files.

Let's first do a quick sanity check. We'll alter a file in one directory, check it in, and then ask Subversion to update our local copy in the other directory.

First, edit the file Number.txt in the sesame directory, adding two new lines (*five* and *six*):

```
zero
one
two
three
four
five
six
```

Now check this file into the repository:

```
sesame> svn commit -m "Customer wants more numbers"
Sending        Number.txt
Transmitting file data .
Committed revision 3.
```

Now for the first moment of truth. Over in the aladdin directory, its version of Number.txt is now out-of-date (because the repository now holds a more recent version). Let's pop over there and check:

```
sesame> cd ..
work> cd aladdin
aladdin> svn status --show-updates
        *         2   Number.txt
Status against revision:      3
```

We're using --show-updates (short form -u) to get Subversion to talk to the repository and find out if any updates are available for files in the aladdin directory. We need to use this option because by default Subversion just checks to see whether files in the working copy have been locally modified, not whether an updated version is available in the repository.

The asterisk shows that an update is available for Number.txt, which is currently at revision 2. Subversion also tells us that the repository was at revision 3 when it performed the check.

Before we update to the latest version, we might ask Subversion to tell us what's different between our version of the file and the version currently in the repository (as there are times when you may want to defer an update if it affects stuff you're currently working on). Again, we use the svn diff command:

```
aladdin> svn diff -rHEAD Number.txt
Index: Number.txt
===================================================================
--- Number.txt  (revision 3)
```

```
+++ Number.txt   (working copy)
@@ -3,5 +3,3 @@
 two
 three
 four
-five
-six
```

The -rHEAD option tells Subversion we want to compare our local copy of Number.txt against whatever revision is the most recent in the repository. After another one of those cryptic @@ -3,5 +3,3 @@ lines, we see that the two new lines are missing from our working copy (which shouldn't be a surprise). If we hadn't specified the -r flag, Subversion would compare our local copy of Number.txt against the repository version that was checked out to produce it (r2 in this case). As we haven't altered the file in our Aladdin persona, this would show no changes.

We can update our copy in the aladdin directory to merge in the changes we made over in sesame:

```
aladdin> svn update
U  Number.txt
Updated to revision 3.
```

Subversion prints U next to Number.txt to let us know that it has updated it and tells us that our working copy has been updated to revision 3. If we look at Number.txt, we'll see that we now have the two extra lines.

3.8 Conflict Resolution

So, what happens if two people edit the same file at the same time? It turns out that there are two scenarios. The first is when the changes don't overlap. Simulating this takes a little effort, so hang in there.

First, edit the copy of Number.txt in the sesame directory. Make the first line uppercase:

```
ZERO
one
two
three
four
five
six
```

Now edit the version of Number.txt over in aladdin. This time make the last line uppercase:

Number.txt (in Sesame)

```
zero
one
two
three
four
five
SIX
```

What we've just done is simulate two developers each making local changes to the same file. Right now, these changes are independent, because the repository knows about neither. Let's change that. A coin toss told us that Aladdin checked in his version of the changed file first:

```
aladdin> svn commit -m "Make 'six' important"
Sending        Number.txt
Transmitting file data .
Committed revision 4.
```

A short time later, the *sesame* developer tries to check in too. (Remember, this version of the file has the first line in uppercase.)

```
sesame> svn commit -m "Zero needs emphasizing"
Sending        Number.txt
svn: Commit failed (details follow):
svn: Out of date: '/sesame/trunk/Number.txt' in transaction '7'
```

Subversion is telling us that it tried to commit the change from *sesame*, but it failed because /sesame/trunk/Number.txt is out-of-date. Let's try bringing our local version of the file up-to-date with the repository. Remember that our file has an uppercase *zero*, and the repository version has an upper case *six*.

```
sesame> svn update
G  Number.txt
Updated to revision 4.
```

Subversion prints a `G` to tell us it has merged our changes with the repository version (previously, it printed `U` to let us know it had updated our working copy with a new version from the repository). Let's look at our local version:

```
ZERO
one
two
three
four
five
SIX
```

Magic! Our version now contains *both* our changes and the Aladdin changes. We both edited a file at the same time, and Subversion worked it out.

Before we get too smug, though, remember that our local change (the ZERO) hasn't yet been stored in the repository. We ask Subversion to commit our change, and this time it succeeds, because our local version contains the latest repository revisions:

```
sesame> svn commit -m "Zero needs emphasizing"
Sending        Number.txt
Transmitting file data .
Committed revision 5.
```

The next time Aladdin updates, he'll get our changes too:

```
sesame> cd ..
work> cd aladdin
aladdin> svn update
U  Number.txt
Updated to revision 5.
```

Butting Heads—When Changes Clash

In the previous example, the changes made by the two (virtual) developers didn't overlap. What happens if two developers edit the same lines in the same file at the same time? Let's find out.

Go into the sesame directory and change the second line in Number.txt from *one* to *ichi*. Don't check this change in. Now go across to the aladdin directory and change the same line from *one* to *uno*. Let's assume that once again Aladdin gets to check in his changes first:

```
aladdin> svn commit -m "User likes Italian one"
Sending        Number.txt
Transmitting file data .
Committed revision 6.
```

Now let's go back to the sesame directory. Remembering that we're supposed to be simulating two separate users, we pretend we don't know about the changes made by Aladdin, and so try to check in our changes:

```
sesame> svn commit -m "One should be Japanese"
Sending        Number.txt
svn: Commit failed (details follow):
svn: Out of date: '/sesame/trunk/Number.txt' in transaction 'c'
```

We've seen this message before: we need to update to get the repository changes:

```
sesame> svn update
C  Number.txt
Updated to revision 6.
```

Subversion tells us it has managed to update Sesame's working copy to revision 6, but the C next to Number.txt tells us that there was a conflict when it tried to merge the repository changes with our local changes. Have we lost all our hard work? No.

CVS Hint: When CVS detects a conflict, it'll print a whole bunch of warning messages and generally tell you the sky is falling. This is to remind you to fix the conflict, as it's very easy to check in a file that still has conflict markers left in it. Subversion tracks the file's state so it knows whether you've resolved the conflict, and won't let you check in until things are okay.

When conflicts happen, it's most often because two developers had some kind of misunderstanding. In this case, one developer wanted to change the line to Italian, and the other wanted Japanese. If you think about this, it becomes apparent that what we have here is a breakdown in communication; there's a problem in the team (or at least in the team's process). Whatever the cause, we're left wondering, "what should the line really be?" Subversion doesn't have a hot line to the truth, so it can't solve the problem. Instead, it adds special annotations to the file to show what the conflict is. In this case if we look at the file Number.txt, we'll see it now looks like:

```
ZERO
<<<<<<< .mine
ichi
=======
uno
>>>>>>> .r6
two
three
four
five
SIX
```

The lines with the <<<<<<< and >>>>>>> show where the conflict occurred. Between them we can see both our change *and* the conflicting change in the repository. Time to do some detective work. The first thing we need to do is to find out who made the change in the repository. We'll use svn log to help us find out what happened here. The conflict markers seem to suggest r6 is causing the problem:

```
sesame> svn log -r6 Number.txt
------------------------------------------------------------
r6 | mike | 2004-09-08 23:01:03 -0600 (Wed, 08 Sep 2004)

User likes Italian one
------------------------------------------------------------
```

Looking at the log entry, we can see the name of the author of the change, along with their checkin comment. We wander over and ask him about the change. A quick call to the customer resolves the problem: the customer wanted the word *one* in Japanese, and *two* in Italian. Aladdin must have misheard. Armed with this new information, we can now resolve the conflict. Edit Number.txt in the sesame directory, remove Subversion's conflict markers, and make the changes requested by the customer:

```
ZERO
ichi
due
two
three
four
five
SIX
```

Having removed the conflict markers, we can tell Subversion we've resolved the conflict and then commit the file:

```
sesame> svn resolved Number.txt
Resolved conflicted state of 'Number.txt'
sesame> svn commit -m "One is Japanese, two Italian"
Sending        Number.txt
Transmitting file data .
Committed revision 7.
```

Subversion actually helped us discover a misunderstanding. We resolved the conflict, and everyone is happy. Optimistic locking may actually deserve its name. And, just to make things even less scary, we need to emphasize that conflicts rarely happen on real projects.

However, it's also worth noting that Subversion is not a mind-reader. It might happen that two people fix the same bug in two different ways. If these changes don't conflict at the source code level, Subversion will happily accept both, even though it may make no sense to have both fixes in the same code. The lack of a conflict means you haven't trodden on anyone else's changes at the textual level, but you should still rely on unit tests to verify that the change works.

That's all for our quick tour around Subversion. However, you may want to leave your test repository lying around. Later, you might find it helpful if you want to experiment with a particular facility before doing it for real in the project repository.

Chapter 4

How To...

Even though version control sounds great in theory, many teams don't use it. Sometimes this is because the theory doesn't seem to translate into practice too well. It's all very well reading a document that says something like "generate a release branch," but what does that actually mean when it comes down to typing in the correct Subversion commands?

Another problem is that teams sometimes embrace version control too vigorously, creating very complex structures to hold their source, with correspondingly frightening lists of instructions for achieving even the simplest task. The result? Eventually (and in our experience that means very quickly), the team gives up; using the version control system is seen to be just too much hassle.

The remaining chapters in this book address both of these problems. They present a simple way to organize your version control system and a set of basic practices for doing the everyday things a team needs to do. We suggest to start you use these basic practices as a set of recipes; follow them whenever you need to achieve a certain result. Try hard not to deviate too much from them; if you find yourself wanting to create a scenario we don't cover, think hard before proceeding. Perhaps you don't really need it.

As with any set of recipes, you'll soon find yourself feeling more and more comfortable following them. This is the time to start some gentle experimenting. However, we suggest you don't try something new directly in a real project's repository.

Instead, set up the scenario in a test repository (such as the one we set up in the previous chapter), and try things out there.

4.1 Our Basic Philosophy

We think version control is one of the three essential technical practices; every team needs to be proficient in all three (the others are *Pragmatic Unit Testing* [HT03] and *Pragmatic Project Automation* [Cla04]). Every team should be using version control—all the time, and for everything they produce. So we have to make it simple, obvious, and lightweight (because if we don't, people will eventually stop doing it).

Simplicity means that doing something that *should* be simple will actually be simple. Checking in all out changes is a simple (and common) operation, so the basic operation should be one or two actions. Creating a new customer release is a somewhat more complex concept, so it's okay to use a few more steps doing it, but it should still be as simple as possible.

Version control has to be *obvious*: we need to arrange things so that it is clear what we're doing and what version of the software we're doing it to. There should be no guessing when it comes to the source.

Finally, we're describing a *lightweight* process; we don't want version control to get in the way of getting real work done.

4.2 Important Steps When Using Version Control

Here is our basic set of rules for organizing your source in a Subversion repository:

- Before you start, you need to establish an effective and secure way to access your repository.

- Once you've gained access, there is a simple set of Subversion commands that you'll be using daily.

- Each project that your company develops must be stored in a distinct directory within the Subversion repository.

You should be able to check out a project's complete source from a single point.

- If projects contain subcomponents that can be worked on in isolation, or if you intend to share components between projects, these components should be stored as projects in their own right and included as an external resource in other projects.

- If your project incorporates code from third parties (vendors, or perhaps open-source projects) you need to manage this as a resource.

- Developers should use branches to separate the main line of development from code lines that have different life cycles, such as release branches and major code experiments. Tags are used to identify significant points in time, including releases and bug fixes.

We cover each of these topics in the chapters that follow.

## Chapter 5

Accessing a Repository

In Chapter 3, *Getting Started with Subversion*, on page 27, we created a repository and learned how to access it via a file-based URL. This is great for a single user but doesn't really help a whole development team collaborate properly. In this chapter we'll discuss the three main ways you can make an existing repository available over the network, what they mean for a user accessing a repository, and the pros and cons of the various access mechanisms.

Appendix A on page 147 includes a guide for administrators who are installing, networking, and securing Subversion.

5.1 Network Protocols

After creating our sandbox repository, we used a *repository URL* to tell Subversion what we wanted to check out. This URL included both a definition of where the repository was and also what path inside the repository we were interested in. Once we had a working copy we didn't need to keep using the repository URL, since Subversion remembers where our working copy came from.

repository URL

Repository URLs are important whenever we want to directly access a repository (when we're creating branches and tags or merging big sets of changes, for example). Figure 5.1 on the next page shows how the URL for our sandbox repository is composed.

The first part of this URL is file. This specifies the *scheme* we're using to locate the repository, in this case the local

scheme

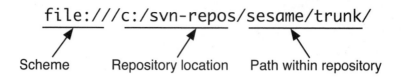

Figure 5.1: COMPONENTS OF A REPOSITORY URL

filesystem. The next part, `c:/svn-repos`, tells Subversion the repository database files are in a particular directory on the C: drive. Finally, `/sesame/trunk/` specifies the path within the repository that we're interested in.

Subversion supports a number of different schemes in repository URLs and even allows you to define custom extensions yourself. Each different scheme tells Subversion to access the repository via a particular network protocol. We'll start by looking at the simple `svn` protocol.

svn

The easiest way to network a repository is to use the `svn` scheme. Subversion comes with svnserve, a small server that listens for network connections, allows repository access over the network, and supports simple authentication of users. svnserve is probably most suitable for teams on a private LAN who want to get going quickly.

If an administrator (possibly you!) has used the instructions in Section A.2, *Networking with svnserve*, on page 148 to put the Sesame repository online, you can check it out by running

```
work> svn co svn://olio/sesame/trunk vizier
A  vizier/Number.txt
A  vizier/Day.txt
Checked out revision 7.
```

Success! We used the svn scheme to access a repository on a machine called `olio`, and we checked out the Sesame project to a new vizier working directory.

If you've tried playing with the working copy on your client machine, you might find that Subversion doesn't let you commit any changes. For example, try adding a new data file, Month.txt, to the project:

```
vizier> svn add Month.txt
A         Month.txt
vizier> svn commit -m "Added month data"
svn: Commit failed (details follow):
svn: Connection is read-only
```

If this happens, your administrator has forgotten to enable write access to the repository (it's read-only by default). Get them to look at Section A.5, *svnserve*, on page 159 and set up some users. Once they've done this, you should be asked for a username and password when you try to commit a change:

```
vizier> svn commit -m "Added month data"
Authentication realm: <svn://olio:3690> sesame/trunk
Password for 'mike':
Adding          Month.txt
Transmitting file data .
Committed revision 8.
```

Subversion decided to try username `mike` because that's my username on the client machine. If this isn't right, just hit Enter at the password prompt, and Subversion will let you specify a different username.

svn+ssh

svnserve does a great job of getting a repository up on the network, but it has a couple of drawbacks. Firstly, although passwords are never transmitted in clear text over the network, the *contents* of your files travel unencrypted. Anyone who can sniff your network traffic can see what your files contain. This might be okay for a team all on the same LAN, but if you want to use the public Internet for accessing your repository it simply isn't secure. Secondly, passwords are stored in plain text in the server's conf directory and can only be changed by an administrator with access to the password file.

Subversion solves both of these security problems by leveraging the *Secure Shell* (SSH). If you're a Unix user, you might   *Secure Shell* already have SSH infrastructure in place for connecting to your server. SSH employs strong encryption to protect the contents of a client-server session. It is widely used for administering servers over the Internet. Figure 5.2 on the following page shows how Subversion secures an svn connection using SSH.

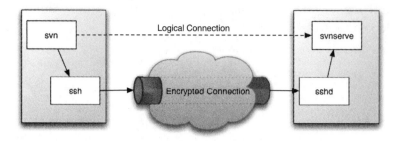

Figure 5.2: TUNNEL SUBVERSION OVER SSH

Subversion needs an SSH client installed on your machine in order for you to access a repository using svn+ssh. Unix users are likely to have SSH already installed, but if you're on Windows, you'll need to do a bit of work. Putty is an excellent SSH client and is available from http://www.chiark. greenend.org.uk/~sgtatham/putty/. Download plink.exe, and save it somewhere in your path; C:\Windows\system32 usually works. If you're using TortoiseSVN you don't need to worry about installing an SSH client since Tortoise comes with TortoisePlink.

Next you need to edit your Subversion client configuration settings. Windows applications store user-specific data inside a special folder, which changes location depending upon how your computer is set up and which version of Windows you're using. If you're not sure where your application data directory is, open a command prompt and run the following:

```
work> echo %APPDATA%
C:\Documents and Settings\mike\Application Data
```

Once you've found your application data directory, open the Subversion subdirectory, and edit the config file that's inside. Edit the section on tunnels so it looks like this:

```
[tunnels]
ssh=plink
```

You need to specify a svn+ssh scheme if you'd like Subversion to use SSH to protect your connections. If your server accepts SSH connections, try running

```
work> svn checkout  \
         svn+ssh://olio/home/mike/svn-repos/sesame/trunk  \
         princess
mike@olio's password:
A  princess/Month.txt
A  princess/Number.txt
A  princess/Day.txt
Checked out revision 8.
```

This looks just like the repository URL we used earlier with svnserve, except we changed the scheme to svn+ssh. If you're having problems accessing your repository, Section A.3, *Troubleshooting an SSH Connection*, on page 151 contains a guide to diagnosing the problem.

Subversion is now using SSH to open a connection to the server and authenticate you as a Unix user. Subversion uses the standard Unix user and group permissions to determine whether the user with which we connect has permission to access the repository. If you're using SSH public/private keys or an SSH agent to manage your credentials, the Subversion client automatically takes advantage of this, which might mean you don't get asked for a password at all.

Using svn+ssh is appealing if you already have SSH accounts for your users, because you can leverage all your existing infrastructure. The extra security lets you connect over the Internet without fear that someone might steal your Sesame project code and without all the hassle of setting up a full VPN. svn+ssh is a straightforward solution that should have you up and running pretty fast.

http

Subversion can also host a repository over the web by using the Apache web server. A special Subversion module, called mod_dav_svn, does the hard work and allows Subversion to share the web server with traditional web sites. Apache is highly configurable, and Subversion takes full advantage of its built-in security and scalability. You can host a repository using standard http and https and leverage any of the authentication mechanisms already supported by Apache.

You may have heard that Subversion *requires* Apache—this actually isn't true; neither svn nor svn+ssh need anything extra to network your repository. Most prebuilt Unix packages have a dependency on Apache because they install all three networking options, which is where the misunderstanding comes from. Using Subversion with Apache is probably the most popular solution for sharing a repository over the Internet.

Apache provides a wealth of authentication options for users. From basic authentication using password files to integration with a Windows domain or an LDAP server, Apache is supremely flexible. You can even set up directory-based security, dividing your repository into read-only or even completely private sections. You can take advantage of standard SSL certificates for encrypting connections to the server and avoid firewall hassles by using standard web server port numbers.

To access a repository hosted by Apache on server `olio`, use the following command:

```
work> svn checkout  \
        http://olio.mynetwork.net/svn-repos/sesame/trunk  \
        sesame
Authentication realm: ... Subversion repository
Password for 'mike': ******
A  sesame/Month.txt
A  sesame/Number.txt
A  sesame/Day.txt
Checked out revision 8.
```

This particular repository requires an authenticated user even for read-only access. Subversion automatically tries username `mike`; if that's wrong just, hit Enter instead of typing a password, and Subversion will let you specify the username.

5.2 Choosing a Networking Option

All three network protocols for Subversion (`svn`, `svn+ssh` and `http`) offer different trade-offs in terms of ease of setup, security, and administration overhead. Which you choose will depend on what kind of infrastructure you already have, your security needs, and your familiarity with Apache.

It's important to note that the networking option you choose today doesn't have to be the one you stick with tomorrow. Networking a repository simply puts it on the network—you can change between svnserve and Apache (for example) as often as you like. It's also possible to support multiple different access mechanisms *at the same time*, although you have to be careful with permissions.

If your team is on a reasonably secure LAN, or even a larger network connected by a VPN, using the simple svnserve server and svn protocol is a quick way to get up and running with Subversion. You'll have some administrative overhead when adding new users or changing passwords, but this should be offset by the easy startup.

If you already have existing SSH infrastructure in place, using svn+ssh makes a lot of sense. You get strong crypto protecting your connections and can take advantage of all of the key-management and authentication options that SSH provides. Make sure your Unix administrator understands how groups, umasks, and sticky bits need to be set up before proceeding, though.

If you want to host a repository over the Internet, leverage Apache's wide range of authentication mechanisms, or simply play with the big boys and run a "real" server, using Apache to host your Subversion repository is the way to go. You'll be able to use SSL and client-server certificates for encryption and verifying you're really talking to whom you think you're talking to, and you'll be able to authorize users using a Windows domain, LDAP, or any other authentication mechanism that Apache supports. You'll also be able to be much more precise about which parts of a repository users have access to, by leveraging Apache's built-in access controls. Using Apache on standard HTTP ports also means fewer holes need to be opened on your firewalls. Your network administrator will thank you for that.

Chapter 6

Common Subversion Commands

In Chapter 3, *Getting Started with Subversion*, on page 27 we created a simple project and experimented with basic Subversion commands. In this chapter we'll take this further by presenting a set of recipes: the Subversion commands that you use to do everyday tasks.

This section is not exhaustive. Later in this book we'll be looking at more advanced issues, such as release management, workspaces, and third-party code. However, the commands and techniques in this chapter should handle 90 percent of the work you do with Subversion.

These examples assume you have your repository up and running and that you've enabled network access. We'll assume the Sesame project's main code line (the trunk) is located at svn://olio/sesame/trunk. You'll need to use your own server name instead of olio and the right access scheme if you're using http or svn+ssh instead of the basic svn.

6.1 Checking Things Out

The svn checkout command (often abbreviated co) gets Subversion to create a new working copy from a directory stored in the repository. In its simplest form, the checkout command creates a working copy in a directory with the same name as the repository directory:

```
work> svn checkout svn://olio/sesame/trunk
A   trunk/Month.txt
A   trunk/Number.txt
A   trunk/Day.txt
Checked out revision 8.
```

Here, Subversion created the working copy in a local trunk directory, because that's the name of the directory in the repository. This might not be what you want, especially if you're following the conventions recommended in Chapter 7, *Organizing Your Repository*, on page 101. You can use an extra argument when checking out to specify the name of the directory Subversion should use for your working copy:

```
work> svn checkout svn://olio/sesame/trunk sesame
A   sesame/Month.txt
A   sesame/Number.txt
A   sesame/Day.txt
Checked out revision 8.
```

By default, Subversion checks out the latest revision stored in the repository. If you'd like an older version, use the -r option to specify the revision number or date you'd like. Section 6.6, *Using Subversion Revision Identifiers*, on page 81 contains full details on how to refer to a particular revision.

To check out a copy of the Sesame project before we added Month.txt, we can specify revision 7:

```
work> svn checkout -r 7 svn://olio/sesame/trunk old-sesame
A   old-sesame/Number.txt
A   old-sesame/Day.txt
Checked out revision 7.
```

If you're like us, you'll probably end up with a bunch of different working copies in your work directory. To figure out where a working copy came from, use the svn info command:

```
work> svn info sesame
Path: sesame
URL: svn://olio/sesame/trunk
Repository UUID: d6959e13-a0e3-0310-8d55-a8c2e0b5e323
Revision: 34
Node Kind: directory
Schedule: normal
Last Changed Author: mike
Last Changed Rev: 7
Last Changed Date: 2004-10-05 13:07:15 -0700 (Tue 5 Oct 2004)
```

The important bit here is the URL on the second line. Subversion is telling us that the sesame directory on the local machine originally came from svn://olio/sesame/trunk/.

6.2 Keeping Up-to-Date

If you're not the only person working on a project, the chances are pretty good that the repository is being updated by others even as you are working. It's a good idea to incorporate their changes into your working copy fairly frequently; the longer you leave it, the bigger the hassle of fixing any conflicts.[1] We typically update our working copies every hour or so throughout the day.

The svn update command is used within a working copy and brings all the files the directory (and its subdirectories) up-to-date with the repository. Files and directories added to the repository will be added to the working copy, and files and directories removed from the repository will be removed from the working copy. The following command updates the working copy of the Sesame project:

```
work> cd sesame
sesame> svn update
```

You can choose to update just part of your checked-out tree. If you issue the command in a subdirectory of a project, then only files at or below that point will be updated. This may save time, but it also leaves you exposed to working on an inconsistent set of files.

You can also specify one or more individual files or directories to update by naming them on the command line:

```
main> svn update build.xml src/ test/
```

During the update process, Subversion will show the status of each file with significant activity. For example, the following is the logging produced when updating the directory tree containing the Subversion source code itself:

```
subversion> svn update
U   include/svn_repos.h
G   libsvn_client/status.c
A   bindings/java/javahl/build
A   bindings/java/javahl/build/build.xml
U   bindings/swig/perl/native/Repos.pm
```

---

[1]Frequent merges serve another purpose. If another developer is going down the wrong path, or if their changes are promising to be problematic in the long term, you'll find out sooner if you merge often. The earlier you get this feedback, the less the pain involved in fixing the problem.

```
U  bindings/swig/perl/native/Fs.pm
U  bindings/swig/perl/native/Wc.pm
U  bindings/swig/perl/native/Base.pm
A  bindings/swig/perl/native/Makefile.PL.in
UU bindings/swig/perl/native/h2i.pl
U  bindings/swig/perl/native/Ra.pm
D  bindings/swig/perl/native/Makefile.PL
 U bindings/swig/perl/native
U  clients/cmdline/propedit-cmd.c
A  po/pt_BR.po
U  po/zh_TW.po
Updated to revision 11141.
```

Subversion prints the following characters to indicate what has happened to each file or directory:

- A indicates Subversion has added a file to your working copy in order to bring it up-to-date with a new file in the repository.

- U shows a file that was out-of-date in your working copy because a newer version was checked into the repository. Subversion has updated your working copy of the file to the new version.

- D indicates that Subversion has removed a file from your working copy because the file has been deleted from the repository.

- G shows a file that was out-of-date in your working copy, which you had modified locally. Subversion successfully merged the changes from the repository with your local modifications.

- C shows a file that was out-of-date in your working copy, which you had also modified locally. Subversion tried to merge the changes from the repository with your local modifications but encountered a conflict. You'll need to resolve the conflict before you can check in.

You might have noticed the line Subversion printed for h2i.pl starts with UU and that the line for the bindings/swig/perl/native directory has a space followed by a U. These aren't typesetting errors—Subversion is actually printing two columns of information. The second column indicates changes to a file's *properties*, rather than to a file itself. Subversion properties are discussed in more detail in Section 6.4, *Properties*, on the next page.

6.3 Adding Files and Directories

The svn add command tells Subversion to add files and directories to the repository. When you add a directory, Subversion automatically adds all the files within the directory and its subdirectories, unless you specify the --non-recursive option:

```
sesame> mkdir timelib
sesame> cd timelib
timelib> # ..create and edit Time.java..#
timelib> cd ..
sesame> svn add timelib
A        timelib
A        timelib/Time.java
```

Note that at this point Subversion has just remembered the names of the files you'd like to add to the repository; it hasn't actually added the files or made the change visible to anyone else. You need to use svn commit to commit the new files into the repository.

Subversion stores all files in the repository in a binary format, using an efficient binary-delta algorithm to figure out what has changed between revisions. This works great for text as well as real binaries, so you don't need to tell Subversion if a file is binary when adding it to the repository.

Subversion treats text and binary files differently as we'll see in Section 6.4, *Setting Mime Types*, on page 74, which means it's sometimes worth checking that Subversion detected the "binaryness" of a file correctly. When you add a file that Subversion thinks is binary, it'll automatically set the svn:mime-type property to `application/octet-stream`. The next section covers properties in detail.

6.4 Properties

Whilst we are mostly concerned with Subversion storing file *contents* it can also store metadata associated with each file (and directory) in the repository.[2] Subversion calls this metadata *properties* and manages changes to properties in the *properties* same way as a file's contents. Properties can be changed

---

[2]Subversion actually stores properties on *revisions* too. For example, the log message associated with a particular commit is stored in a text property on the revision.

by different users and are updated in each working directory when users run svn update. This can lead to merges and conflicts just like those encountered when changing file contents.

Properties are named using simple strings and can contain any content that a normal file could contain—this specifically includes binary content. Properties can be used to associate extra data with a file, in whatever format you'd like. For example, a Java source file could have an associated Reviewer property that tells you who last performed a code review on that file. A repository storing music files might have a short sample of each file stored in a binary property, rather than storing the samples in files alongside the main file and using some naming convention to link the two.

You can use Subversion's properties however you like, but you should be aware of a few special properties. These properties change the way Subversion behaves when it encounters a file, and all start with the svn: prefix.

Manipulating Properties

To set a property on a file, use the svn propset command:

```
sesame> svn propset checked-by "Mike Mason" Number.txt
property 'checked-by' set on 'Number.txt'
sesame> svn status
 M     Number.txt
```

Here we're setting the checked-by property on Number.txt to value Mike Mason. Maybe our project's release procedure requires each of our files to have this property set so that we can figure out who approved the contents. It's important to note that we're making a change to the file's properties, which Subversion handles in the same way as a change to the contents. Subversion records the file in our local copy as modified, and we must commit the change to the repository if we want anyone else to see it.

To edit a property, use svn propedit. This will bring up an editor so that you can easily manage multiline text properties:

```
sesame> svn propedit checked-by Number.txt
        # .. edit the property, then save and quit the editor ..
Set new value for property 'checked-by' on 'Number.txt'
```

The svn proplist and svn propget commands list all the properties for a file and print out the current value of a property:

```
sesame> svn proplist Number.txt
Properties on 'Number.txt':
  checked-by
sesame> svn propget checked-by Number.txt
Mike
Ian
```

Finally, you can use svn propdel to delete a property entirely. Remember that the property is not lost forever—Subversion tracks changes to properties just like changes to files, so you can always go back in time and find any previous revision.

Keyword Expansion

If you've used another version control system, you may be familiar with *keyword expansion*. This basically means getting your version control system to modify your working copy files as it checks them out and updates them so it can fill in useful information for you. Each of these useful pieces of information is represented by a *keyword*, usually surrounded by dollar signs, which you put strategically inside the files you're storing in version control. Keywords in Subversion are stored unexpanded in the repository to make diffing and merging a little easier.

keyword expansion

keyword

We really recommend *not* using this Subversion feature, since it can get you into lots of bother. We tried to make this page of the book perforated so readers could tear it out and forget all about keyword expansion, but our publishers said it'd add too much to the production costs....

To switch on keyword expansion, you need to set svn:keywords on each file containing keywords. The property value should list the keywords you'd like to expand for that particular file. Subversion offers the following keywords:

$LastChangedDate$

>   Also abbreviated $Date$, this keyword describes the last time the file was committed to the repository. It expands to a string such as 2004-09-26 18:11:03 -0700 (Sun, 26 Sep 2004).

$LastChangedRevision$

>   Also known as $Revision$ or Rev, this keyword expands

to the revision number the last time the file was committed to the repository.

$LastChangedBy$

Also abbreviated $Author$, this keyword expands to the name of the last user to have committed the file.

$HeadURL$

Also abbreviated URL, this keyword expands to the full URL of the file in the repository.

Id

This keyword expands to a short summary of the other keywords, suitable for use in a file's header section.

Let's suppose we want to turn on keyword expansion for the file Number.txt in our Sesame project. First we need to set svn:keywords to the list of keywords we want to expand:

```
sesame> svn propset svn:keywords "HeadURL Id" Number.txt
property 'svn:keywords' set on 'Number.txt'
```

Now edit Number.txt, and add two header lines with the keywords we want expanded. Here we're using $HeadURL$ and Id:

```
# $HeadURL$
# $Id$
ZERO
ichi
due
three
four
five
SIX
```

Now when we commit our changes, Subversion will notice that we've asked for keyword expansion and modify the working copy file. Each keyword is expanded to the latest information Subversion has for the file:

```
sesame> svn commit -m "Added file keywords"
Sending        Number.txt
Transmitting file data .
Committed revision 10.
sesame> cat Number.txt
# $HeadURL: svn://olio/sesame/trunk/Number.txt $
# $Id: Number.txt 10 2004-09-27 00:09:05Z mike $
ZERO
ichi
due
three
four
five
SIX
```

 Joe Asks. . .

Where's the Log keyword?

The keywords available in other version control systems, including CVS, often include a Log keyword. This expands to list all of the log messages ever used when committing changes to the file.

The practical problem is that all this extra stuff in the source files gets in the way of reading the code. We've seen source with two or three full pages of log messages at the top of it, all before you get to a single line of real code. Code is there to be read, and anything that gets in the way of reading it is bad.

The philosophical problem is that you're duplicating information. Everything that can be inserted using keywords is already stored within Subversion (it has to be; otherwise Subversion couldn't add it in the first place). So why not just go to the horse's mouth and ask Subversion directly? That way you'll get authoritative information that's guaranteed to be up-to-date.

The Subversion developers think the use of keywords, especially anything that includes verbose possibly long commit messages, should not be encouraged. The result is they haven't included a Log keyword.

Keyword expansion really doesn't have many benefits, and it has several drawbacks. We recommend not using it.

Whilst writing this book using the Pragmatic Programmers' CVS-based system, Mike got caught out by the expansion of Log and Id keywords and had to switch it off for various chapters. The irony of using CVS to write a Subversion book is not lost on him.

Editor's note: Mike's book moved us so deeply that we now do book production using Subversion.

autoprops

If you want to use keyword expansion on lots of files, say, all your .java files, that's a lot of property setting to remember to do. Fortunately, Subversion has a feature called *autoprops* that can set properties for you. Autoprops are explained in detail in Section 6.4, *Automatic Property Setting*, on page 75.

Ignoring Certain Files

Most of the time your working copy will contain both files you want under version control (source code, build scripts, graphics for your application, and so on) and files that you're happy to have lying around but that don't need to be stored in the repository (temporary files, compiled code, and logfiles). Some Subversion commands, notably svn status, svn add, and svn import assume you're interested in all the files in your working copy. For example, svn status displays files that aren't under revision control in case you've forgotten to add them.

This extra output for files you really don't want Subversion to worry about can be annoying, or just plain dangerous (try accidentally adding a few large temporary files to your repository, and see if your administrator comes running your way with a big stick...). Fortunately, there's an easy way to avoid these problems: setting the svn:ignore property on a directory specifies files you'd like Subversion to ignore.

Suppose we've been working on the time library in our Sesame project. Ask Subversion for a status report, and we might see:

```
sesame> svn status timelib/
?       timelib/Time.class
?       timelib/Time.java.bak
M       timelib/Time.java
```

Here we can see that we've changed Time.java but that Subversion is also reporting on Time.class and Time.java.bak, neither of which we actually care much about.

Use svn propedit svn:ignore timelib to bring up an editor for the svn:ignore property on timelib. Enter the following contents:

```
*.class
*.bak
```

Now running svn status will ignore the .class and .bak files:

```
sesame> svn status
 M      timelib
 M      timelib/Time.java
```

The timelib directory is listed as modified because we changed its svn:ignore property.

Once your changes are committed, everyone will receive the update to the svn:ignore property on timelib, causing Subversion to ignore files in their working copies too. The svn:ignore property applies only to the contents of a particular directory; it doesn't apply recursively to subdirectories.

Setting End-of-Line Style

Computer systems store text files using a combination of normal characters—the alphabet, numbers, and so on—and special *control characters*. A combination of up to two of these are used to denote the end of a line of text. Depending on the operating system, a computer will use a carriage-return followed by a linefeed (CRLF, used by Windows computers), simply a linefeed (LF, used by Unix and Mac OS X), or sometimes just a plain carriage-return (CR, used by older versions of Mac OS).

control characters

If you're storing files that should be usable on clients where the line-ending style differs, you might be worried about how line endings are stored. Subversion stores all files, whether they're text, graphics, compiled object code, or movies, using a binary format in the repository. Unless you ask it to, Subversion will never convert a file's line-ending style, which might mean you can ignore this section entirely.

If you do need to share files across different operating systems, you may already have noticed strange behavior. Opening a Unix-formatted file using Windows' Notepad, for example, produces a file with lots of little squares in it instead of newlines. Opening a Windows-formatted file in Unix might result in lots of ^M characters at the end of each line.

Whilst your editor or IDE might claim to be able to do conversions for you, or to maintain the end-of-line style that exists in a file when editing it, we often find the best thing is to stick with native linefeed formats for each operating system. Subversion will do a conversion for you if you set the svn:eol-style property to one of the values in the following table.

native   Subversion will translate end-of-line characters to whatever the client operating system expects, and so will use CRLF on Windows and LF on Unix.

CRLF   Subversion will always use CRLF as an end-of-line marker when it creates files in the working copy.

LF   Subversion will always use LF as an end-of-line marker on the client.

CR   Subversion will always use CR as an end-of-line marker on the client.

Setting Mime Types

Setting the svn:mime-type property on a file tells Subversion exactly what type of content a file has. Mime types are used a lot on the Internet—especially by e-mail and web servers—to describe files that are being transferred around or sent as e-mail attachments. For example, XML documents have a mime type of *text/xml*, JPEG graphics are of type *image/jpeg*, and Microsoft Word documents have an *application/msword* mime type.

Setting svn:mime-type on a file is useful for a couple of reasons.

Firstly, Subversion assumes files that don't have a text mime type (starting *text/*) have binary contents, so it should treat them differently on the client when merging and displaying diffs. A diff on a binary file probably won't be human readable, so Subversion skips trying to show you a diff and just tells you the file has changed. A merge on a binary file is equally unlikely to work very well, so when you're receiving changes from the repository to a binary file you've changed in your working directory, Subversion renames *your* version of the file with a .orig file extension and replaces your file with new data from the repository.

Secondly, when Subversion is being used with Apache as its network server, you can browse the repository using a normal web browser. When you click on a link, Subversion uses the svn:mime-type property to figure out what the type of the file should be when Apache returns it to your web browser. This helps avoid seeing a screenful of binary data when you click on a zip file in the repository.

Executable Flags

Some operating systems, most notably Unix, treat simple data files differently than program files. To be able to run a program on Unix it must have its "execute bit" set. If you're checking executable files or scripts into your repository, users checking the files out won't automatically get the execute bit set. Setting the svn:executable property on a file means that Subversion will set the execute bit for you whenever that file is checked out. It doesn't matter what the property is set to—if it's set at all, Subversion will set the execute bit.

On Windows, all files are executable, so you probably won't have to worry about this.

Automatic Property Setting

Subversion properties are very useful, but unfortunately they need to be applied to each file or directory we're interested in. It's easy to forget to set a property, and that might lead to problems later.

Fortunately, Subversion includes a feature called *autoprops* that allows you to specify properties that should be added automatically. For example, you might decide that .java files should have svn:keywords set to *LastChangedDate* and have svn:eol-style set to *native*. You might also decide that whenever someone adds a .gpg file to the repository it should have its svn:mime-type set to *application/pgp-encrypted*.

Autoprops are a client-side setting, so if you want all your developers to use them you'll need some kind of policy for making sure everyone is set up correctly. Unfortunately, Subversion doesn't (yet) have the ability to "broadcast" configuration settings from the server to clients, so you'll have to do this by hand.

Subversion stores your settings in a user-specific application data folder. Where this actually is depends on whether you're using Unix or Windows. Section 5.1, *svn+ssh*, on page 57 covers finding the folder on Windows, and on Unix Subversion uses ~/.subversion.

Edit Subversion's config file, and uncomment the following line:

```
enable-auto-props = yes
```

Next scroll down a little, and uncomment the autoprops section, adding whatever properties you'd like to set. To enable a mime type on .gpg files and native end-of-line style on .java files, you'd want a section like this:

```
[auto-props]
*.java = svn:eol-style=native
*.gpg = svn:mime-type=application/pgp-encrypted
```

6.5 Copying and Moving Files and Directories

Subversion remembers every file and directory you ever commit to the repository. This is great in most cases, but if you make a mistake and add a file to the wrong directory, or add it with the wrong name, you might want to move or rename something. Modern programming includes a technique called *refactoring*, which often involves renaming a program file when you come up with a better name for what that file does or a more logical location for it in your project.

Fortunately, Subversion includes copy and move commands allowing you to move and rename[3] files and directories. Subversion's history tracking also knows about these operations, so it's much better to move a file using a Subversion command than to move it yourself manually.

Copying a File

Whilst you could manually copy a file using Windows Explorer or the Unix cp command, then add the new file to version control, Subversion provides the svn copy command to allow copying of files.

---

[3]A "rename" is just a "move" that happens to move a file to the same directory. Unix gurus will probably be able to explain exactly why this makes sense, but Subversion's move and rename commands do the same thing.

Copying is *the* fundamental operation in Subversion upon which everything else is based. Successive revisions of a file are copies of the file with the contents changed. Branches are copies of entire directories to a new location. Tags are copies of a set of files that provide a snapshot of the repository at a particular point in time.

Given that copying is such an epic activity, why would you want to do it just to add another copy of a file to your repository? Ultimately you might not, but when you copy a file using svn copy, Subversion can track the history of both the original and the copy back to the same source. In fact, Subversion doesn't even store a complete copy of the file; it just stores a reference to where it was copied from. This might be useful if you have a lot of big files that came from the same source and have just been changed a little.

Enough evangelism. Using svn copy is a good idea, and it works like this:

```
sesame> svn copy Number.txt Data.txt
A         Data.txt
sesame> svn commit -m "Created example data file"
Adding         Data.txt
Committed revision 24.
```

Copying a file or directory creates copies in your local working directory and schedules them for addition to the repository. A normal svn commit will check them in and complete the copy.

Since Subversion remembers the shared history of the files, asking for the log for Data.txt also gives us the history for the file Number.txt:

```
sesame> svn log Data.txt
------------------------------------------------------------
r24 | mike | 2004-11-17 16:00:37 -0700 (Wed, 17 Nov 2004)
Created example data file
------------------------------------------------------------
r11 | mike | 2004-10-04 21:05:37 -0600 (Mon, 04 Oct 2004)
Added Ian as reviewer
------------------------------------------------------------
r10 | mike | 2004-09-26 18:09:05 -0600 (Sun, 26 Sep 2004)
Added file keywords
------------------------------------------------------------
r7 | mike | 2004-09-08 23:22:06 -0600 (Wed, 08 Sep 2004)
One is Japanese, two Italian
------------------------------------------------------------
```

Renaming a File

Let's suppose that our Sesame project's Time.java has actually become more of a "clock" class and that we'd like to rename it. We could rename the file in our working copy using Windows Explorer or the Unix mv command, then use svn delete to delete Time.java and svn add to add Clock.java, but that won't allow Subversion to track the file history for us.

First let's examine the history for Time.java:

```
timelib> svn log Time.java
------------------------------------------------------------
r14 | mike | 2004-10-04 21:12:48 -0600 (Mon, 04 Oct 2004)
Added freeze/unfreeze time methods
------------------------------------------------------------
r13 | mike | 2004-10-04 21:10:50 -0600 (Mon, 04 Oct 2004)
Added getCurrentDate() method
------------------------------------------------------------
```

Our most recent change to the file, adding methods for freezing and unfreezing the system time, really means that our class would be better named Clock. We know that things can get out of hand if we don't name our classes well, so we decide to make the change sooner rather than later. Use the svn move command to rename the file:

```
timelib> svn move Time.java Clock.java
A         Clock.java
D         Time.java
```

Here Subversion is letting us know that our "move" is really an add and a delete. Someday Subversion may support renames as first-class operations, but for the moment a Subversion move is stored in the repository as a history-aware copy from the old name to the new name and a delete of the old name.

Before you get all excited and commit the change, you should crank up your unit tests and make sure you didn't break anything. At the very least, this Java file now won't compile because it contains a Time class in a file called Clock.java. Open your favorite editor, and change the class name to Clock. Then make sure your tests pass. You might need to change code that references the class so it uses the new name too.[4]

---

[4]Renaming a Java file requires quite a few steps, as does a rename in other programming languages. Fortunately, some development environments integrate directly with version control and will perform all the renames, adds, and deletes for you automatically. Check your IDE for "refactoring support."

What's in a Name?

Subversion's move command can also be referred to as svn mv, rename, and ren. The svn copy command can be shortened to svn cp if you're into the whole brevity thing.

While we're on the subject of naming, it's worth pointing out that naming *things* (classes, variables, methods, tests, data files, machines, processes, etc.) is both really difficult and really important. Most people don't name stuff completely right the first time around, but a well-named object helps avoid misunderstanding and speeds communication. Once you realise there's a better name for something, make the effort to rename it. Your colleagues will thank you!

Once everything is working, commit your changes:

```
timelib> svn commit -m "Renamed Time to Clock"
Adding          timelib/Clock.java
Deleting        timelib/Time.java
Transmitting file data .
Committed revision 15.
```

Now if we view the history for the new Clock.java, we'll see the hard work has paid off, as Subversion follows the history of the file across the rename:

```
timelib> svn log -v Clock.java
------------------------------------------------------------
r15 | mike | 2004-10-04 21:13:40 -0600 (Mon, 04 Oct 2004)
Changed paths:
   A /sesame/trunk/timelib/Clock.java
               (from /sesame/trunk/timelib/Time.java:14)
   D /sesame/trunk/timelib/Time.java
Renamed Time to Clock
------------------------------------------------------------
r14 | mike | 2004-10-04 21:12:48 -0600 (Mon, 04 Oct 2004)
Changed paths:
   M /sesame/trunk/timelib/Time.java
Added freeze/unfreeze time methods
------------------------------------------------------------
r13 | mike | 2004-10-04 21:10:50 -0600 (Mon, 04 Oct 2004)
Changed paths:
   M /sesame/trunk/timelib/Time.java
Added getCurrentDate() method
------------------------------------------------------------
```

Renaming a Directory

With Subversion, directories are first-class objects just like files. We can happily move or rename a directory using the svn move command. Maybe the time library has had a few extra utilities added to it and should be renamed util.

```
timelib> cd ..
sesame> svn move timelib util
A       util
D       timelib/Clock.java
D       timelib
sesame> svn commit -m "Renamed timelib to util"
Deleting      timelib
Adding        util
Adding        util/Clock.java
Committed revision 16.
```

Using Repository URLs

The svn move command we've seen so far has been running on the working copy—moves, renames, adds, and deletes happen on the client before being committed to the server. This is appropriate in most cases, because program code often usually need to be edited after being moved so that the code will still compile and the tests will still pass.

Subversion also allows you to run these commands using a repository URL, without the need for a working copy at all. The changes are made instantly in the repository and require a commit message. It might be appropriate to use this kind of renaming if you have a lot of big files and don't want to move them around using a working copy. If you're moving *code*, however, think twice—you won't be able to run your tests without a working copy and might well break stuff.

To perform a repository-based rename, use two URLs like the one initially used for a checkout. Let's rename the util directory common instead:

```
work> svn move -m "Renamed util to common" \
        svn://olio/sesame/trunk/util      \
        svn://olio/sesame/trunk/common
Committed revision 17.
```

Back in the Sesame working copy, performing an update will get the new common directory and delete the old util directory:

```
sesame> svn update
A  common
A  common/Clock.java
D  util
Updated to revision 17.
```

6.6 Seeing What Has Changed

The svn diff command shows you the differences between versions of files. You can compare the version of a file in the repository with your locally modified copy, and you can see the differences between two versions of a file in the repository.

Seeing What You've Changed in Your Working Copy

The simplest use of svn diff is to show you what you've changed since you last updated your working copy from the repository:

```
common> svn diff Clock.java
Index: Clock.java
===========================================================
--- Clock.java   (revision 21)
+++ Clock.java   (working copy)
@@ -20,6 +20,11 @@
               frozen = true;
       }
+       public static void setTime(long time)
+       {
+               frozenTime = time;
+       }
+
        public static void unfreezeTime()
        {
               frozen = false;
```

Here we can see that we last updated to revision 21 of the file Clock.java and that since then we added the setTime() method.

The basic svn diff command shows the changes between the file in your workspace and the version to which you last updated. Subversion can do this without contacting the server because it stores a pristine, local copy of each file in your working directory. If someone else has changed the file and committed their changes into the repository, however, you won't see them in the diff. We'll see how to handle this shortly.

Using Subversion Revision Identifiers

We looked at Subversion's -r option when checking out and updating, and it turns out referring to revisions is something we'll be doing a lot with Subversion. The option you supply after -r is called a *revision identifier*. When you're using a revision identifier, Subversion will accept revision numbers, dates, and a few symbolic names, shown in the following table.

revision identifier

number   A revision number within the repository, for example 87.

{ date }   A revision at the start of the date, for example {"2004-09-26 13:35:06"}. The curly braces tell Subversion you're using a date, and the quotes are required if you're using a date format containing spaces. Subversion supports a variety of date formats, including the basic HH:mm denoting a particular time on today's date.

HEAD   The latest revision stored in the repository.

BASE   The base revision of an item's working copy—this is the revision you last checked out or updated to.

COMMITTED   The last revision in which an item changed at or before BASE.

PREV   The revision just before COMMITTED.

revision range

Some commands accept a *revision range*, which is simply two revision identifiers separated by a colon. Revision ranges are used to refer to two revisions separated over time.

The symbolic revisions BASE, COMMITTED, and PREV can be used only to refer to an item in a working copy, because they don't make sense otherwise.

Figure 6.1 on the next page shows Subversion's symbolic revisions. In this scenario, you have revision 2 of Graph.java in your working copy, and another developer checks in some changes, creating revision 3 in the repository. Since you haven't updated your working copy, the BASE revision for your copy of Graph.java is revision 2. The PREV revision is one earlier than this, namely revision 1. HEAD is always the newest version in the repository, in this case revision 3.

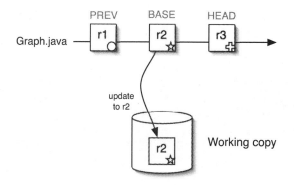

Figure 6.1: SYMBOLIC REVISIONS FOR A WORKING COPY FILE

Finding Differences between Versions

To compare two revisions of a particular file, use the -r option to specify a revision range:

```
common> svn diff -r19:21 Clock.java
Index: Clock.java
===========================================================
--- Clock.java   (revision 19)
+++ Clock.java   (revision 21)
@@ -1,9 +1,11 @@
 package timelib;

+import java.util.Date;
+
 public class Clock
 {
-    private boolean frozen = false;
-    private long frozenTime = 0;
+    private static boolean frozen = false;
+    private static long frozenTime = 0;

     public static Date getCurrentDate()
     {
```

Here we used a file in the working copy to produce the diff, even though a working copy doesn't contain historical information. Under the hood, Subversion translates the file path into a repository URL so it can retrieve the older versions. If you don't have a working copy, you can diff directly against the repository:

```
common> svn diff -r19:21   \
         svn://olio/sesame/trunk/common/Clock.java
Index: Clock.java
===========================================================
--- Clock.java   (revision 19)
```

```
+++ Clock.java  (revision 21)
@@ -1,9 +1,11 @@
 package timelib;
+import java.util.Date;
+
 public class Clock
 {
-    private boolean frozen = false;
-    private long frozenTime = 0;
+    private static boolean frozen = false;
+    private static long frozenTime = 0;

    public static Date getCurrentDate()
    {
```

Earlier we noted that a common gotcha with svn diff is that it doesn't show changes that have happened in the repository. To get Subversion to compare your working copy against the latest revision in the repository, use the HEAD keyword:

```
common> svn diff -r HEAD Clock.java
Index: Clock.java
===============================================================
--- Clock.java  (revision 26)
+++ Clock.java  (working copy)
@@ -1,6 +1,7 @@
 package timelib;
 import java.util.Date;
+import java.util.Calendar;
 public class Clock
 {
@@ -24,6 +25,11 @@
        frozenTime = System.currentTimeMillis();
    }
+    public static void switchToGMT()
+    {
+        frozenTime -= Calendar.getInstance()
+                            .get(Calendar.ZONE_OFFSET);
+    }
+
    public static void setTime(long time)
    {
        frozenTime = time;
@@ -38,10 +44,5 @@
    {
        frozen = false;
    }
-
-    public static boolean isFrozen()
-    {
-        return frozen;
-    }
 }
```

In our working copy of Clock we've added the switchToGMT() method. Meanwhile, another developer added the isFrozen()

method and checked in. When we ask for a diff against HEAD, we can see our local changes as additions and the other developer's changes as *deletions*—if we check in Clock.java exactly as it is in our working copy, we'll undo the change adding isFrozen(). Fortunately, Subversion won't let us do this—we'll need to update before checking in, which will add the isFrozen() method to our working copy.

Sometimes it's useful to see the most recent change to a file before you start working on it. You can do this by using the PREV symbolic revision:

```
common> svn diff -r PREV:BASE Clock.java
Index: Clock.java
===========================================================
--- Clock.java   (revision 22)
+++ Clock.java   (working copy)
@@ -26,6 +26,11 @@
         frozenTime = time;
    }
+    public static void setTime(Date date)
+    {
+        frozenTime = date.getTime();
+    }
+
    public static void unfreezeTime()
    {
        frozen = false;
```

Here Subversion is showing us that the previous change to Clock.java was the addition of the setTime() method.

Subversion's diff command can also examine changes between different development branches or show you what changed since a certain version of the code was tagged. Chapter 8, *Using Tags and Branches*, on page 105 covers diffing and merging across tags and branches.

Diffs and Patch

If you've spent any time in the open-source community, you'll have come across folks flinging source patches around the world. These patches are based on the same diffs that Subversion generates, which turns out to be remarkably useful.

Perhaps you're working with an open-source library, and you need to make a change. The library is hosted on CodeHaus,[5]

---

[5]http://codehaus.org/

which among other things provides free Subversion repositories for open-source developers. As a member of the public, CodeHaus lets you check the source code of the project out of the repository, but because you aren't on the list of developers, you can't check changes back in.

This is where patches come in. Simply ask Subversion to give you a list of all the changes you've made (using svn diff). E-mail the file containing the diff output to the library's maintainer, who will be able to use the patch program to apply those patches to their source.

The following command creates a file called mychanges.patch containing all the changes that have been made to files in or below the directory oslibrary:

```
oslibrary> svn diff > mychanges.patch
```

You can then e-mail this file to the maintainer, who can apply the patch to his or her version of the source using (suprise!) the patch command:

```
oslibrary> patch -p0 -i mychanges.patch
```

Correct use of patch is a mystic art that probably cannot be taught in a book this size, but here's a rough breakdown of what's going on:

- The patch is being applied in oslibrary, *the same directory* in which it was created.

- The -p0 option is instructing patch to strip zero directories from files named in the patch before applying it. If you don't include this option, patch will complain about being unable to find the right files.

- The -i option is telling patch to use mychanges.patch as input.

patch is pretty clever and can usually ignore "garbage" text surrounding a patch, so you can save an e-mail containing someone's changes and apply the whole thing. What most people forget is the magic -p0 that lets patch find the right files.

Patches are useful outside the context of open source. You can use patches to send suggested changes to other members of your project team. If your clients have your source code, you can even use patches to distribute those urgent three-in-the-morning fixes that seem to crop up from time to time. Just remember to check in the changes you've made into the repository as well.

6.7 Handling Merge Conflicts

Subversion doesn't lock files:[6] everyone in a project can edit any file at any time. This feature of Subversion seems to give some people sleepless nights. "What stops two people editing the same file at the same time?" they ask. "Won't work get lost?" The simple answers are "nothing, and no." If they edit different parts of that same file, Subversion will happily merge the two changes together, and life carries on.

Sometimes, however, two people edit the *same* parts of the same file (although it happens far more rarely than you might first think). When that happens, Subversion cannot automatically perform a merge: it wouldn't know whose changes to keep. In these cases, Subversion declares that the two versions of a file conflict and passes the matter back to a human (you) to solve.

To illustrate a conflict, we'll use our old friend Numbers.txt again. This time, we'll check it out into two separate working directories:[7]

```
work> svn checkout svn://olio/sesame/trunk sesame1
A  sesame1/Number.txt
A  sesame1/Day.txt
Checked out revision 1.
work> svn checkout svn://olio/sesame/trunk sesame2
A  sesame2/Number.txt
A  sesame2/Day.txt
Checked out revision 1.
```

---

[6]Subversion 1.2 will support optional locking with a feature called *reserved checkouts*.

[7]Eagle-eyed readers will notice these examples take us back to revision 1 of the repository, when we had only two files and no timelib directory. This was possible through some Subversion administration magic—we made a backup of our repository including just revision 1 and loaded the backup into a new repository. Section A.6, *Backing Up Your Repository*, on page 164 covers this magic in detail.

In the sesame1 directory, we'll change the first line of Numbers.txt so that it contains the following:

```
ZERO
one
two
```

We'll check this change in:

```
sesame1> svn commit -m "Made zero uppercase"
Sending        Number.txt
Transmitting file data .
Committed revision 2.
```

Now we'll bop over to sesame2. Remember that we want to create a merge conflict, so we'll pretend that we don't know that someone changed the file we're about to work on. In sesame2 we'll alter Numbers.txt, changing the first line to read Zero:

```
sesame2> svn commit -m "Capitalized 'Zero'"
Sending        Number.txt
Transmitting file data .svn: Commit failed (details follow):
svn: Out of date: '/sesame/trunk/Number.txt' in transaction '9'
```

So far, so good. Subversion has detected that Number.txt is out-of-date, so we do an svn update:

```
sesame2> svn update
C  Number.txt
Updated to revision 2.
```

Subversion marks the file with a C to let us know there's a conflict in the merge, and it's our job to fix it.

Fixing a Conflict

The first question to be answered when fixing a merge conflict is, "why did this happen in the first place?" This isn't an issue of blame, but it often is one of communication. What are two developers doing editing the same lines of code in the same file at the same time?

Sometimes there's a good reason. Perhaps they both discover the same bug at the same time, and both decide to fix it. Or perhaps they're both adding functionality which uses a common data structure, and both add fields to that structure at the same time. These are reasonable changes, and they might lead to a conflict.

But often conflicts happen because folks aren't doing a good job of letting others know what's going on. So, we strongly recommend that if you come across a merge conflict without a sensible explanation you make a point of mentioning it at the next team meeting. The goal here is to discuss the cause and to come up with ways of improving communication so that the chances of something similar happening in the future are reduced.

Now that's all fine, but you're still left with a conflict. Subversion marks these in the local copy of the file using sequences of $<<<$ and $>>>$ characters:

```
<<<<<<< .mine
Zero
=======
ZERO
>>>>>>> .r2
one
two
```

Here we can see our change, `Zero`, helpfully labeled `mine`, and the change from the repository, `ZERO`, with the hint that it came from revision 2.

We now have to decide how to fix this. In the real world, this involves a negotiation with the other person who made the change; simply blowing their hard work away and replacing it with yours is a great way to jeopardize your invitation to the next project picnic.

The resolution could go a number of ways:

- You decide to scrap your changes and use the version in the repository. All you have to do is svn revert your changes—Subversion will back out your change and use the version of the file from the repository:

  ```
  sesame2> svn revert Number.txt
  Reverted 'Number.txt'
  sesame2> svn update Number.txt
  At revision 2.
  ```

- You decide to keep your changes and lose those in the repository. Subversion saves a copy of each version of the file when a conflict arises, with extensions .mine, .r1, .r2, etc. Copy your version of the file, the one with the .mine extension, over the original, and tell Subversion you've fixed the conflict:

  ```
  sesame2> cp Number.txt.mine Number.txt
  sesame2> svn resolved Number.txt
  Resolved conflicted state of 'Number.txt'
  ```

Conflicts and Curly Brace Wars

Suppose two developers like to lay their code out differently. Fred likes his code indented with two spaces and likes all his curly braces to sit on the same line as a declaration. His code would look like this:

```
for (i = 0; i < max; i++) {
  if (values[i] < 0) {
    process(values[i]);
  }
}
```

Wilma, however, likes her code indented with four spaces and doesn't appreciated the cluttered look of Fred's code. She puts her curly braces on a different line to declarations. If Wilma were writing the same piece of code, it would look like this:

```
for (i = 0; i < max; i++)
{
    if (values[i] < 0)
    {
        process(values[i]);
    }
}
```

One day Fred is editing some of Wilma's code and decides he dislikes the indentation. He tells his editor to reindent the whole file to two-character offsets and to put the curly braces where he likes them. He then makes a small change to one line, saves the file, and commits the changes to the repository.

The problem is that as far as Subversion is concerned, every line in the file has changed. If Wilma (or anyone else) changes something, they'll get a merge conflict, because Fred's change to the indentation means that the corresponding line in the repository is different from the line in Wilma's workspace.

Now you can get around this: you can tell Subversion to use an external diff program that ignores changes in whitespace when determining the difference between files, for example. However, this doesn't get around the fact that you have changed the whole file and that folks with local changes to that file will get conflicts the next time they update.

Conflicts and Curly Brace Wars (continued)

The rule is simple: don't wantonly change the layout of a shared file. If you absolutely must change the indentation, first make sure no one else on the team has made local changes to the file. Then change the layout and check in the changed file, without changing anything else. Then tell folks to update, so they'll all be working on the new version. This'll cut down on the number of conflicts people experience, and will reduce the amount of hate mail you receive.

Subversion will clean up all the various .mine and .r2 files when you tell it you've resolved the conflict.

- If you decide you want to use parts of both versions, then you'll need to do some manual editing. Simply edit the file that contains the conflict markers, making it look the way you want. Be sure to remove the conflict markers. For example, in our case we might decide that the first line shouldn't be Zero or ZERO but Empty:

```
<<<<<<< .mine                          Empty
Zero                                   one
=======          becomes =>            two
ZERO
>>>>>>> .r2
one
two
```

Subversion won't let you commit a file that is still in a conflicted state.[8] In order to let Subversion know you've fixed a conflict, use the svn resolved command:

```
sesame2> svn resolved Number.txt
Resolved conflicted state of 'Number.txt'
```

---

[8]This is probably reassuring for folks who have big projects and lots of files—"What if I don't see a C next to a file as it scrolls past my screen?" is a common question. If you miss the conflict, and by some chance having a bunch of <<< characters in your code doesn't horribly break your build, Subversion will complain about any files remaining unresolved when you try to commit.

6.8 Committing Changes

After you make a set of changes (and, in an ideal world, after you've tested they don't break anything), you'll want to store them in the repository. We've already done this many times in this book; you simply use svn commit.

However, we'd like to recommend a slightly more complex sequence of commands to follow at every commit:

```
myproject> svn update
myproject> #... resolve conflicts ...
myproject> #... run tests ...
myproject> svn commit -m "check in message"
```

The first line brings our local workspace into step with the current state of the repository. This is important; although our code may work fine with the project files as they were when we last updated our workspace, other folks may have changed things that break our new code. After updating, we might have to resolve conflicts.

Even if there are no conflicts, we should compile and test our code again, fixing any problems that arise. This ensures that when we do check in we'll be checking in something that actually works in the larger project context. You'll need a fast test suite for this to work—developers won't want to hang around more than a few minutes while their tests run.

Once we've checked that everything is correct, we can commit our changes, using the -m option to add a meaningful message. If you omit the -m option, Subversion will bring up an editor and let you type in a longer comment.

6.9 Examining Change History

You can look at the log messages that you and your team have entered using the svn log command:

```
sesame> svn log Number.txt
------------------------------------------------------------
r4 | mike | 2004-09-08 22:45:16 -0600 (Wed, 08 Sep 2004)
Make 'six' important
------------------------------------------------------------
r3 | mike | 2004-09-08 22:05:32 -0600 (Wed, 08 Sep 2004)
Customer wants more numbers
------------------------------------------------------------
r1 | mike | 2004-09-08 21:50:13 -0600 (Wed, 08 Sep 2004)
------------------------------------------------------------
```

Meaningful Log Messages

What makes a good log message? To answer this question, imagine you are another developer coming to this code base a couple of years from now. You are puzzling over a particular piece of the system, trying to work out why something is done a certain way. You notice that changes were made in this area, and hope that the log messages will give you hints as to the motivation for the particular design chosen.

Now, back to the present. What little breadcrumbs can you drop into the log messages today to help your fellow developers a couple of years from now?

Part of the answer comes from realizing that Subversion already stores the actual details of the changes you made to the code. There's no point in writing a log message that says "changed timeout to 42." when a simple diff could show that `setTimeout(10)` became `setTimeout(42)`. Instead, use the log message to answer the question "why?":

```
If the round-robin DNS returns a machine that
is unavailable, the connect() method attempts
to retry for 30mS. In these circumstances our
timeout was too low.
```

If a change is being made in response to a bug report, include the tracking number in the log message: the description of the problem is already in the bug database and doesn't need to be repeated here.

If you'd just like to get a general idea of what has changed recently, you can ask Subversion for a log of everything that happened in a particular directory. Doing this at the top of a large tree might produce quite a bit of output, so use a pipe[9] through the more command to paginate Subversion's output:

```
work> svn log sesame | more
```

Subversion will accept a -r option to specify which revisions you're interested in. Using a single revision number will show just what changed in that revision, and using a revision range will show a section of history:

```
sesame> svn log -r 19:24 Clock.java
------------------------------------------------------------
r19 | mike | 2004-10-04 21:47:09 -0600 (Mon, 04 Oct 2004)
Renamed util to common
------------------------------------------------------------
r21 | mike | 2004-10-09 16:33:00 -0600 (Sat, 09 Oct 2004)
Fixed compilation problems
------------------------------------------------------------
r22 | dave | 2004-10-09 16:48:23 -0600 (Sat, 09 Oct 2004)
Added setTime() method
------------------------------------------------------------
r23 | ian | 2004-10-09 17:00:23 -0600 (Sat, 09 Oct 2004)
Added setTime() method taking a Date
------------------------------------------------------------
r24 | dave | 2004-10-10 18:07:08 -0600 (Sun, 10 Oct 2004)
Added Log class
------------------------------------------------------------
```

Here we asked to see revisions 19 through 24 of Clock.java. We didn't actually change Clock.java in revision 20 of the repository, which is why we're missing a revision here. Also notice how Subversion printed the revisions with the newest at the bottom—retrieving a log without using the -r option prints the newest revision at the top.

The final message says "Added Log class" but is being shown as part of the history for Clock.java. This looks a bit strange, so let's get more information using the -v (verbose) option:

```
common> svn log -r 24 -v Clock.java
------------------------------------------------------------
r24 | dave | 2004-10-10 18:07:08 -0600 (Sun, 10 Oct 2004)
Changed paths:
   M /sesame/trunk/common/Clock.java
   A /sesame/trunk/common/Log.java
Added Log class
------------------------------------------------------------
```

---

[9]The pipe character is Shift+\ on a U.S. keyboard.

Now that Subversion is being more talkative, we can see that revision 24 added Log.java and also made a change to the file Clock.java. In this case, the new Log class depends on some extra functionality in Clock. When Dave committed his change, he committed both the files at once, since they make logical sense together.

Subversion's ability to track changes to multiple files in a single commit is extremely powerful. If you're browsing history for a particular file and see a change you're interested in, adding the -v option to svn log will show all the files that were changed in that particular commit. This comes in handy when tracking down what needed to be changed for a particular bug fix, for example.

Line-by-Line History

The svn blame[10] command displays the contents of one or more files. For each line in each file it shows the latest revision number to change that line, along with the author of the change:

```
sesame> svn blame Number.txt
    10       mike # $HeadURL$
    10       mike # $Id$
     5       dave ZERO
     7       mike ichi
     7       mike due
     1       mike three
     1       mike four
     3       andy five
     4       ian  SIX
```

This is a great tool when you're involved in software archeology; you can quickly find the patterns to changes and identify exactly which lines were changed by a particular revision.

svn blame accepts a -r option specifying a revision or revision range to use when displaying the file. This stops Subversion from examining the entire history of the file when displaying annotations.

---

[10]It's called *blame* because it's often used to determine who is responsible for a particular piece of code (or a particular bug!). svn blame, praise, annotate and ann all mean the same thing.

6.10 Removing a Change

Sometimes we make changes to code that we'd rather forget.

If the change is a set of changes in our local workspace that have yet to be checked in, then we can simply throw the changes away using svn revert.

CVS Hint: CVS users will be used to simply deleting a file with local modifications and then doing an update to restore the file. Whilst this will work with Subversion too, doing an actual revert is safer and faster—an update will contact the server and possibly pull down new changes that you're not ready to receive.

If the change is already committed, Subversion can help us remove it. There are a number of ways of doing this; here we'll show a sequence of steps that we consider to be the simplest and least error prone. For this example, let's assume we're working on a contact management system. We've been making preliminary releases to beta sites, and things have been going well until a client phones up in a panic; when they removed a client contact from their address list, it removed all the client's information from the database too.

The first step is to make sure we're up-to-date.

```
contacts> svn update
U  Contacts.java
Updated to revision 28.
```

Then we identify the exact revision we want to remove. svn log is useful for this. Let's have a look at the log for the main contact manager class:

```
contacts> svn log Contacts.java
------------------------------------------------------------
r28 | mike | 2004-10-11 10:54:08 -0600 (Mon, 11 Oct 2004)
Reformat PMB Addresses
------------------------------------------------------------
r27 | fred | 2004-10-11 10:52:47 -0600 (Mon, 11 Oct 2004)
Remove from database too
------------------------------------------------------------
r26 | ian | 2004-10-11 10:51:38 -0600 (Mon, 11 Oct 2004)
Sort clients into alpha order (Bug 2942)
------------------------------------------------------------
```

Revision 27 looks suspicious, so we use svn diff to see exactly what changed between revisions 26 and 27:

```
contacts> svn diff -r 26:27 Contacts.java
Index: Contacts.java
===================================================================
--- Contacts.java       (revision 26)
+++ Contacts.java       (revision 27)
```

```
@@ -25,6 +25,7 @@
    public void removeClient(Client client)
    {
+       database.deleteAll(client);
        clientList.remove(client);
    }
 }
```

This looks like the problem. However, before we start wantonly hacking someone else's change, let's do some investigating. Looking at the log, we see that this particular change was made by Fred, so we wander over and chat. It turns out that this was a simple misunderstanding; Fred hadn't realized that the call would delete all the client records. It's okay to remove the change.[11]

We now have to remove the changes to Contacts.java that were made in revision 27. We use the svn merge command to back out the change:

```
contacts> svn merge -r 27:26 Contacts.java
U  Contacts.java
```

We're asking Subversion to calculate the changes between revisions 27 and 26 for Contacts.java and apply those changes to our working copy. We used revision range 27:26 because we'd like to *reverse* the change. We can use svn diff to verify that Subversion has correctly undone the change:

```
contacts> svn diff Contacts.java
Index: Contacts.java
===========================================================
--- Contacts.java         (revision 28)
+++ Contacts.java         (working copy)
@@ -26,7 +26,6 @@
    public void removeClient(Client client)
    {
-       database.deleteAll(client);
        clientList.remove(client);
    }
```

At this point, we're back into a normal flow. We've made a change to the source, so we should test it then commit the change to the repository:

```
contacts> svn commit -m "Revert deleteAll change from r27"
Sending        contacts/Contacts.java
Transmitting file data .
Committed revision 29.
```

---

[11]It would also be prudent to do a quick search of the rest of the code to see if Fred has used the deleteAll() call in other places.

Reverting Bigger Changes

The recipe we just showed was for reverting changes to a single file. How can we handle changes that involve many files?

Fortunately, Subversion tracks all the files we changed in each commit; as long as changes are grouped together in logical chunks, they're easy to undo. If r27 had actually been a change to a bunch of different files in the contacts directory, we can undo all those changes by using . (the current directory) as the target:

```
contacts> svn merge -r 27:26 .
U  Contacts.java
U  Database.java
```

It's very important to commit related changes together in a single revision. If a single logical change, such as "add date of birth field," is spread over several commits, it becomes more difficult to revert the change and also more difficult to track which files the change touched. When browsing history, you can use the -v (verbose) option to list all the files that changed in a particular revision.

The svn merge command also allows you to specify repository URLs when merging. We'll be using this in Chapter 8, *Using Tags and Branches*, on page 105 for merging changes between branches.

Checking Your Workspace

You work in your local working copy, editing files and adding new files (and occasionally deleting files too). At the same time, other folks on your team are doing the same thing, checking their changes into the repository. As a result, it's easy to lose track of the state of your working copy. In particular, a common problem is forgetting to add new files in your working copy to the repository.

The svn status command can get information about the files in your working directory:

```
proj> svn status
?       common/Calendar.java
M       contacts/Contacts.java
```

Here Subversion is telling us that Calendar.java is in our working directory but that it hasn't not been added to version control. We can also see that we've modified Contacts.java.

By default Subversion just displays information about your working copy and doesn't need to hit the network to do so. If someone else has changed a file in the repository and we're out-of-date we won't know about it. However, Subversion will talk to the server and display extra information if you specify the --show-updates option (you can use -u if you're trying to avoid RSI):

```
proj> svn status --show-updates
?                       common/Calendar.java
        *       26      common/Log.java
M       *       27      contacts/Contacts.java
Status against revision:        30
```

Now we know that both Log.java and Contacts.java are out-of-date in our working copy. We have revision 26 of Log.java and revision 27 of Contacts.java (which we've also modified). The repository is currently at revision 30, and when we do an update, we'll get those extra changes incorporated into our working copy.

## Chapter 7

Organizing Your Repository

When using a version control system, you'll most likely want to store more than one project. A single Subversion repository can be used to store files used by developers across an organization, whether those developers are working on the same team or not. Version control systems use a variety of techniques for splitting a repository into projects, subprojects, modules, and so on. Subversion uses a fairly simple mechanism, organizing everything into directories.

7.1 A Simple Project

Throughout this book, we've been using the Sesame project as our main example. Back in Section 3.3, *Creating a Simple Project*, on page 33, we imported our Sesame project files to /sesame/trunk inside the repository. At the time we deferred explanation of why we needed trunk instead of putting files directly in the sesame directory—now it's time to explain a little more.

Most projects will have a *main line* of development, where the majority of development activity occurs. Projects also tend to have *release branches* where code that has been finished and shipped to production is stored. A release branch won't change very much, except for bug fixes that need to be made. Finally, significant events in the life cycle of a project are often recorded in *tags*. A tag might contain the exact code used for releasing version 5 of Sesame, for example.

main line

release branches

tags

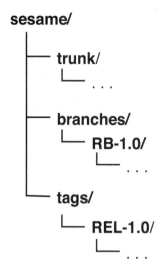

Figure 7.1: THE SESAME PROJECT TRUNK AND BRANCHES

Chapter 8, *Using Tags and Branches*, on page 105 has lots of information about tags and branches, but for now you just need to know that both tags and branches are created by copying directories in the Subversion repository. The recommended location for tags is a *tags/* directory and (suprise!) for branches a *branches/* directory. Both of these directories need to be easy to find for your project, so for Sesame we'd end up with /sesame/trunk for the main development area, /sesame/tags for storing tags, and /sesame/branches for storing branches. Figure 7.1 shows this a little more visually.

7.2 Multiple Projects

So far we have a repository storing the Sesame project. It's easy to see how we could store other projects, Aladdin and Rapunzel, as shown in Figure 7.2 on the facing page.

It's important to realize that because Subversion uses directory copies for branching and tagging, you don't have to name your tags directory *tags*. It might be confusing for your users,

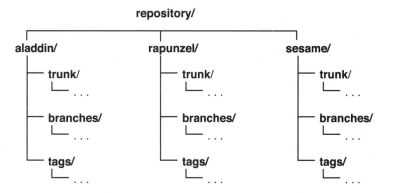

Figure 7.2: ALADDIN AND RAPUNZEL PROJECTS

however, if you're using a different name. You also don't have to put your trunk, tags, and branches directories all together in a single directory. You don't need to have each project at the root directory of the repository—depending on how your developers and IT department are organized, something like /finance/revenue/ali-baba might work best for you.

Subversion's ability to move directories means that if your repository gets out of control—perhaps you have a few dozen projects at the root level and things are getting unwieldy—you can move projects around easily. Using svn move with two repository URLs, as discussed in Section 6.5, *Using Repository URLs*, on page 80, will do a server-side rename and instantly move directories. You should coordinate with developers to make sure they have checked in any outstanding changes, perform the move, and then get everyone to run svn update to get the new directory structure.

7.3 Multiple Repositories

Splitting your projects into different directories makes a lot of sense—developers can easily find the project they should be working on and make changes. It's also possible to split projects across mutliple *repositories*. Since a repository exists on disk as a set of files in a particular directory, you can create multiple repositories in different directories on a single server or create repositories on entirely separate servers.

If you're accessing a Subversion repository using `file://` and `svn+ssh://` URLs, the first part of the URL specifies the path to the repository directory on the server. You can easily change this to specify a different directory for the repository.

When using svnserve, its --root option specifies a *virtual root directory* for your repositories. If you create directories named (for example) repos1 and repos2 inside the virtual root, with a repository in each, these repository directory names become part of the repository URL. In this case you'd access repos1 using `svn://myserver/repos1/`....

If you're using Apache to network a Subversion repository, you might define a virtual directory for each repository on the server. Apache configuration is covered in Appendix A on page 147.

Of course, separating projects across multiple repositories is extra administration overhead—you'll have to back up each repository separately. Users might also need more information on where to find a particular project. The upside to this extra admin overhead is flexibility. If you need to take down a repository for maintenance,[1] you can do so without affecting other repositories. If a particular project is outgrowing the server on which it's hosted, it might make sense to split the repository in two so you can add a second server.

You don't have to make a final decision on day one. Subversion provides tools to allow you to migrate data between repositories, so you can change your mind when you know more about your requirements. To keep things as simple as possible, we recommend using just a single repository until you've got a concrete problem that will be solved by using multiple repositories.

---

[1]This is somewhat unlikely, since most Subversion maintenance, including performing backups, can be done without taking down the server.

Chapter 8

Using Tags and Branches

Day-to-day use of Subversion is pretty simple: you update from your repository, edit files, and save the changes back after you've tested. However, many developers are put off by tags and branches. Perhaps they've worked previously in teams that abused branches and where a diagram of the repository structure would have looked like a bowl of spaghetti rather than a controlled, linear development. Or perhaps they worked in a team where merges between branches were delayed and delayed, so when they did finally occur, it was a nightmare resolving the conflicts. Or perhaps it's just the incredible flexibility that branches offer; with so much choice, it's hard to know what to do.

In reality, tags and branches can (and should) be simple to use. The trick is to use them in the correct circumstances. In this chapter we present two scenarios where we believe branches should be used by teams: generating releases and giving developers a place to experiment.

Beyond these two circumstances, we suggest you think hard before adding branches to a repository. Excessive branching can quickly render any project's repository unusable.

Before we go into the specific recipes, we need to discuss tags and branches in general.

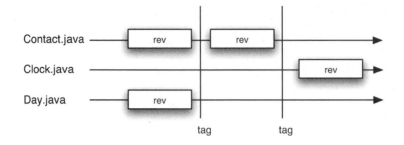

Figure 8.1: TAGS AS SLICES THROUGH THE REPOSITORY

8.1 Tags and Branches

Your Subversion repository probably contains a lot of information. Apart from the sheer number of source files that comprise a typical project, Subversion also stores every revision of each file. Adding time as a dimension to locating information in your repository means the complexity just explodes—how can we possibly keep track of it all? A tag is a symbolic name for a set of files, each with a particular revision number. You can think of a tag as making a slice through your repository and labeling everything inside, as shown in Figure 8.1.

Tags are really useful for keeping track of important events in the life cycle of your project. Instead of having to remember that you built a release for your customer using revision 16 of Calendar.java, revision 23 of Schedule.java, and revision 12 of contacts.dat, you can use a tag to remember this for you. Since a Subversion revision number is also a slice through the repository, you might think we could just use revision numbers or maybe the date we checked the code out in order to build a release. This could work, but tags can also be made from a *mixed revision* working copy—a set of files you've checked out that doesn't correspond to a single repository revision number. This might be needed if you want to pick and choose which versions of project components should be packaged together during a release.

To create a tag in Subversion, copy your code (typically from the trunk) in the *tags* directory for your project. Subversion

---

\\// Joe Asks...
How Do I Make a Tag Read-Only?

Tags are just copies of your repository at a particular revision, so there's nothing to stop people from checking changes into the tags directory. Whilst sometimes it's useful to be able to change a tag, most of the time it's best to treat tags as being read-only.

You can make your tags directory read-only (or more correctly *create-only*—new tags should be allowed) by using one of the repository permissions scripts covered in Section A.5, *Access Control with Hook Scripts*, on page 163. Often, though, this is overkill since developers will be working on the trunk or a release branch, rather than on a tag.

---

handles this copy process very efficiently, making the copy instantly and requiring very little space to store it. The directory to which you copy the code is the symbolic name for the tag. The copy serves as a reference point, storing the files in your project as they were when the tag was created.

Directory copies in Subversion are just that—simple copies. By convention, you'll never make changes to the code stored underneath tags, but there's nothing actually stopping you from doing so. If you *do* check in changes to a tag directory, the tag effectively becomes a branch. Subversion won't move it to your branches directory or anything clever like that, but the tag will no longer contain a fixed snapshot of your repository. This could be useful in certain cases—for example, you could set up a latest tag that always contains your most recently built (and tested) code.

We first talked about branches in Section 2.7, *Branches*, on page 19, when we discussed how we can use them to handle releases in a version control system. A branch represents a fork in the history of the repository; the same file may have two or more sets of independent changes made to it, each set existing in a separate branch.

To create a branch in Subversion, you'll copy your trunk code to a directory underneath branches for your project. The new directory names the branch, and initially just stores a Subversion "cheap copy" of the files as they were when the branch was made. When you check in a change to files on a branch, Subversion remembers the changes in parallel with changes made to the original on the trunk. Subversion also remembers that the two files have a common history.

Tags and Branches in Practice

Tags and branches have many possible uses. However, excessive tagging and branching can end up being remarkably confusing. So to keep things simple, we suggest that initially you use them for four different purposes:

Release Branches

> We recommend putting each release of a project onto a separate branch. The directory used inside branches names the branch.

Releases

> The release branch will contain one (and possibly more) releases: points at which the project is shipped. The release tags identify these points.

Bug Fixes

> Bugs in the release are fixed on the release branch. If appropriate the fix is then merged into the trunck and other release branches. In cases where a bug is fixed in one commit, a Subversion revision number is enough to identify what changed and perform any merges. For more complicated bugs a branch is created for the bug fix and merged into the release branch and trunk when the fix is complete. Tags are created to mark the start and end of the bug fix in order to make merging easier.

Developer Experiments

> Sometimes a subteam has to make far-reaching changes to a project's code base. During the time that these changes are being made, the code is incompatible with the rest of the system and will break the main build. The developers may choose to create a branch labeled as a developer experiment and perform their changes there.

Thing to Name	Name Style	Examples
Release branch	RB-*rel*	RB-1.0 RB-1.0.1a
Releases	REL-*rel*	REL-1.0 REL-1.0.1a
Bug fix branches	BUG-*track*	BUG-3035 BUG-10871
Pre–bug fix	PRE-*track*	PRE-3035 PRE-10871
Post–bug fix	POST-*track*	POST-3035 POST-10871
Developer experiments	TRY-*initials-desc*	TRY-MGM-cache-pages TRY-MR-neo-persistence

Figure 8.2: TAG AND BRANCH NAMING CONVENTIONS

It's a good idea to agree upon a naming convention for tags and branches with your team. The table in Figure 8.2 shows one simple scheme; this is what we'll be using in this book. In this table, *rel* stands for the release number, and *track* is a bug tracking number.

Next we'll take a look at branches and tags in action, starting with a (we hope!) common event in your project life cycle— creating a release branch so we can ship some code.

8.2 Creating a Release Branch

At intervals throughout the life of your software you'll want to generate releases. As the date for each release nears, attention will start to focus away from adding new features, instead concentrating on tidying the smaller release-specific details. Although initially the whole team may participate in this process, there'll come a time when the law of diminishing returns takes effect, and it becomes more efficient to have a release subteam focus on polishing the code for release. If this sub-

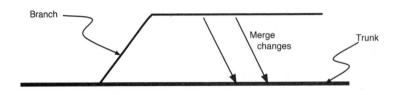

Figure 8.3: RELEASE BRANCH MERGES TO THE TRUNK

team was working in the trunk, the rest of the team would be stalled, waiting for them to finish.

Instead, at this point in the process, move the code to be released into its own branch. While the release team works in that branch, the rest of the project can continue in the trunk. When the release itself is made, we tag the state of the release branch with the release number (remember that a tag is simply a copy of the release branch at a particular point in time). Changes made by the release team in the release branch can then be merged back in to the trunk, as shown in Figure 8.3.

Create the release branch by copying your project's trunk to a new directory underneath branches/. It's best to do this using repository URLs, because then the branch creation will happen entirely on the server and be a lot quicker. You should make sure everyone has checked their local working copy in and is ready for the branch to be created.[1]

In the following example, we create a branch for release 1.0 of our project. We also need to create the /sesame/branches directory, because this is the first branch we've made:

```
work> svn mkdir -m "Creating branches directory"          \
                svn://olio/sesame/branches
Committed revision 32.
```

---

[1]Using repository URLs to create a branch, it's possible to make the branch start from any revision in the repository. If you're a bit late making a branch, it's always possible to talk to other developers, figure out which revision the branch *should* have started at, and use that instead.

```
work> svn copy -m "Creating release branch for 1.0"   \
                   svn://olio/sesame/trunk             \
                   svn://olio/sesame/branches/RB-1.0
Committed revision 33.
```

Both the branches directory creation and the creation of the actual branch require a commit message since they change the repository.

At this point, all we've done is to create the release branch. Any working copies checked out by developers will still be pointing at the trunk. To start actually using the release branch, we'll need to check it out into a new working copy.

8.3   Working in a Release Branch

To access a release branch, you need to check out the project from its branch directory instead of the trunk. You can check out to a separate directory or *switch* an existing working copy to the branch. We recommend the former; it leads to less confusion and simplifies working on both branches at the same time. The svn switch command is useful for assembling different code branches in a working copy, so we'll discuss both methods.

switch

Checking Out a Release Branch

If you're like us, you have plenty of disk space and would rather waste a bit of it than have to remember what branch a particular working copy is looking at. We tend to keep a working copy checked out for each active development branch, just to make things easy.

Change back to your work directory, and then check out from the branch directory overriding the default directory name, so the source will be checked out under the directory rb1.0. When you check out a branch, you are checking out the most recent files in that branch; it's equivalent to the way that checking out in the trunk returns the latest development copies of the files:

```
work> svn co svn://olio/sesame/branches/RB-1.0 rb1.0
A   rb1.0/Month.txt
A   rb1.0/Number.txt
A   rb1.0/common
A   rb1.0/common/Log.java
A   rb1.0/common/Clock.java
```

```
A   rb1.0/Day.txt
A   rb1.0/contacts
A   rb1.0/contacts/Contacts.java
Checked out revision 33.
```

If we now edit a file in this checked-out release directory and commit the changes, Subversion adds the changes into the branch, not into the trunk. We can now continue to refine the files in preparation for the actual release.

Switching a Working Copy to a Release Branch

The svn switch command alters all or part of a working copy so that it points to a different branch. Since most branches contain only a few differences from the trunk, Subversion can do this operation extremely efficiently, transmitting only changed files to the client. Switching a working copy to point at a different branch is much faster than checking out a new working copy for that branch.

To switch your working copy of the Sesame trunk to the 1.0 release branch, run the following svn switch command:

```
work> cd sesame
sesame> svn switch svn://olio/sesame/branches/RB-1.0
U   common/Clock.java
U   contacts/Contacts.java
Updated to revision 36.
```

Subversion updates the files in the Sesame working copy so that they reflect the latest files in the release branch, in this case updating two Java files to reflect bug fixes made on the branch.

The svn switch command also accepts a --revision argument to specify which revision of the branch you'd like to switch to. By default, Subversion switches to the latest revision of the branch (the HEAD revision).

You can switch your working copy back to the trunk like this:

```
sesame> svn switch svn://olio/sesame/trunk
U   common/Clock.java
U   contacts/Contacts.java
Updated to revision 36.
```

Subversion can also switch a subdirectory or even a single file to a different branch. This ability is used in the next section to assemble a working copy with a precise bug fix for a customer.

8.4 Generating a Release

After all the tweaking is over, and the acceptance tests run, the team decides to generate a release. The most important consideration is to ensure that we tag the correct combination of files on the correct branch so that we know precisely what's in the release.

The simplest way to create a release tag is to copy the branch to a new directory under tags. This will tag the latest code in the release branch.

Sometimes you might want to tag files or directories that are not all at the same revision. Generally, wanting to tag anything other than the latest code on a branch is an indication that something has gone wrong somewhere, so we don't advise making a habit of it. Subversion can tag the state of any working copy, copying a mixture of revisions into a tag, from which you can potentially create a release.

These two methods are a little confusing at first, so let's start with the simplest. Once you're happy with the latest code in the release branch, copy it to a new directory under tags:

```
work> svn mkdir -m "Creating tags directory"   \
        svn://olio/sesame/tags
Committed revision 34.
work> svn copy -m "Tag release 1.0.0"          \
        svn://olio/sesame/branches/RB-1.0       \
        svn://olio/sesame/tags/REL-1.0.0
Committed revision 35.
```

The previous svn copy copied the latest code, revision 34 in this case, from the release branch to the new tag REL-1.0.0.

Sometimes you'll need to tag something other than the latest code in a branch. Suppose release 1.0.0 was a couple of months ago, and the team has successfully shipped a bunch of small fixes, taking them to release 1.0.4. An important client requires a fix to release 1.0.0 but doesn't want to wait for 1.0.5 to get the fix. The bug is pretty trivial, so we'd like to add the fix for it to the 1.0.0 code and ship that to the client.[2]

---

[2]This is really a pretty nasty kludge, but if your client really doesn't want to upgrade, it might be the only solution.

We'll check out a working copy with everything as it was in 1.0.0 and then update a few files for our client. In this example, Clock.java contained the bug we're trying to fix:

```
work> svn checkout svn://olio/sesame/tags/REL-1.0.0      \
            client-fix
A  client-fix/Month.txt
A  client-fix/Number.txt
A  client-fix/common
A  client-fix/common/Log.java
A  client-fix/common/Clock.java
A  client-fix/Day.txt
A  client-fix/contacts
A  client-fix/contacts/Contacts.java
Checked out revision 37.
```

Next use svn switch to change where the common directory in your working copy is pointing. We'd like to get the bug fixes from the release branch that have been made since the 1.0.0 tag was created, so we switch and point at RB-1.0:

```
work> cd client-fix
client-fix> svn switch                                   \
          svn://olio/sesame/branches/RB-1.0/common       \
          common
U  common/Clock.java
Updated to revision 37.
```

Now your working copy contains what the client wants—the code as it was when 1.0.0 was shipped, with the critical bug fix that was made on the release branch since then.

After running tests and verifying the code in our working copy does fix the problem, we can create the new tag. We use svn copy to copy our client-fix working copy into a new tag directory REL-1.0.0-clientfix:

```
client-fix> cd ..
work> svn copy -m "Tagging client's 1.0.0 fix" client-fix    \
          svn://olio/sesame/tags/REL-1.0.0-clientfix
Committed revision 37.
```

Developers can retrieve the code used to build a particular release using svn checkout and the tag's URL:

```
work> svn co svn://olio/sesame/tags/REL-1.0.0
A  REL-1.0.0/Month.txt
A  REL-1.0.0/Number.txt
A  REL-1.0.0/common
A  REL-1.0.0/common/Log.java
A  REL-1.0.0/common/Clock.java
A  REL-1.0.0/Day.txt
A  REL-1.0.0/contacts
A  REL-1.0.0/contacts/Contacts.java
Checked out revision 37.
```

8.5 Fixing Bugs in a Release Branch

Bugs happen. The trick is to handle them in a controlled manner. In a release branch, this means we need to keep track of the changes made to fix the bug and then make sure we apply those fixes to every other branch that might contain the same problem. That last point is particularly important. By their nature, branches contain duplicate code. That means if you find a bug in the source code in one branch, there's always the possibility the same bug exists in another branch (after all, originally the source code was the same, bugs and all). In the case of a release branch, we need to be able to apply our fix to the trunk. We might also need to apply it to other release branches (if they also contain the buggy code).

Without version control, this is a tricky problem. With version control, we can manage the process better. We do this by getting the version control system to keep track of the source code changes made while fixing the bug and then merging those changes into the code in other affected branches.

With Subversion, how exactly we track the bug fix depends on how "difficult" the bug is to fix. If it's a small bug, the fix might be a couple of lines changed in a few files. For a more major defect, the fix might involve changing quite a bit of code, and adding and removing some files, and might be a group effort involving more than one developer.

Subversion tracks changes using revision numbers, as we saw in Section 3.6, *Updating the Repository*, on page 39. If you can fix a bug in a single commit, just remembering the revision number is enough for us to copy the change to other branches. If the bug is more complicated and requires several commits to fix (or includes a number of failed attempts to fix it), you might need to create a branch to track the fix.

Simple Bug Fixes

Let's assume we're trying to fix a reasonably simple problem, where the fix just requires changes to a couple of files. The process is described in the following list.

1. Check out the code containing the bug into a local working copy.

2. Generate a test to reveal the bug, fix the code so the new test passes, and verify the build.

3. Commit your changes into the repository, and remember the new revision number. A good way of remembering this revision number is to add it to your bug tracking system so everyone can find it later.

4. Use the new revision number to merge the change to all other affected branches (potentially including the trunk).

As an example, let's fix bug 3065 on the release branch. First we go into the release branch working copy, fix the bug, and check in:

```
rb1.0> # .. edit contacts/Contacts.java and fix the bug .. #
rb1.0> svn commit -m "Fix bug 3065 (address formatting)"
Sending        contacts/Contacts.java
Transmitting file data .
Committed revision 38.
```

Subversion tells us our fix was committed as revision 38. To merge the fix to the trunk, we go to the trunk working copy and ask Subversion to merge revision 38. More specifically, we ask for the difference between revisions 37 and 38 to be merged to the trunk working copy:

```
rb1.0> cd ../sesame
sesame> svn update
At revision 38.
sesame> svn merge -r37:38 svn://olio/sesame/branches/RB-1.0
U  contacts/Contacts.java
sesame> svn commit -m "Merge r38 (fix bug 3065)"
Sending        contacts/Contacts.java
Transmitting file data .
Committed revision 39.
```

Complex Bugs

If you're dealing with a difficult bug that might take several developers a few days to fix, plain old Subversion revision numbers might not cut it. Cheap copies to the rescue once again—we'll create a branch where the bug fixing can be carried out and use tags to identify when we start and finish the fix. These tags will help us merge the fix to other branches. The process works like this:

1. Branch the code containing the bug into a new bug fix branch.

2. Tag the new branch to mark the start of the bug fix.

3. Generate a test to reveal the bug, fix the code so the new test passes, and verify the build.

4. Commit your changes into the repository. If it takes a few tries to fix the bug, don't worry.

5. Once you're happy with the fix, tag the branch again to mark the end of the bug fix.

6. Use the two tags to merge the fix to all the other affected branches.

When creating a branch for the bug fix, we're using the naming convention BUG-*track*, where *track* is a bug tracking number. We use tags named PRE-*track* and POST-*track* to mark the start and end of the bug fix:

```
work> svn copy -m "create bugfix branch"          \
        svn://olio/sesame/branches/RB-1.0          \
        svn://olio/sesame/branches/BUG-10512
Committed revision 40.
work> svn copy -m "tag bugfix start"              \
        svn://olio/sesame/branches/BUG-10512      \
        svn://olio/sesame/tags/PRE-10512
Committed revision 41.
```

We've tagged the start of the bug fix using the tag PRE-10512 and can do the actual bug fixing work in branch BUG-10512. Check out a new working copy of the branch, and fix the bug:

```
work> svn checkout svn://olio/sesame/branches/BUG-10512
A    BUG-10512/Month.txt
A    BUG-10512/Number.txt
A    BUG-10512/common
A    BUG-10512/common/Log.java
A    BUG-10512/common/Clock.java
A    BUG-10512/Day.txt
A    BUG-10512/contacts
A    BUG-10512/contacts/Contacts.java
Checked out revision 41.
work> cd BUG-10512
BUG-10512> # .. Fix bug, possibly adding and removing files .. #
BUG-10512> svn commit -m "Fixing bug 10512"
Adding          Year.txt
Sending         common/Log.java
Transmitting file data ..
Committed revision 42.
BUG-10512> # .. Bug wasn't fixed, ask Bob to help out too .. #
BUG-10512> svn commit -m "Still fixing bug 10512"
Sending         Number.txt
Transmitting file data .
Committed revision 43.
```

At this point we've fixed the bug. It took us a couple of attempts, and maybe we even asked a colleague to check out branch BUG-10512 and take a look at it for us. Now we should tag the bug fix branch so we can identify the end of the bug fix:

```
BUG-10512> cd ..
work> svn copy -m "tag bugfix finish"                    \
         svn://olio/sesame/branches/BUG-10512    \
         svn://olio/sesame/tags/POST-10512
Committed revision 44.
```

Now merge the bug fix to the release branch, which is where we wanted the fix in the first place. After merging, run the test suite to make sure nothing is broken, and then check in:

```
work> cd rb1.0
rb1.0> svn update
At revision 44.
rb1.0> svn merge svn://olio/sesame/tags/PRE-10512    \
                 svn://olio/sesame/tags/POST-10512
U  Number.txt
U  common/Log.java
A  Year.txt
rb1.0> # ... run tests ... #
rb1.0> svn commit -m "Merged fix for bug 10512"
Sending          Number.txt
Adding           Year.txt
Sending          common/Log.java
Transmitting file data ..
Committed revision 45.
```

The same svn merge command can be used to pull the bug fix into other branches and the trunk. Just change into your trunk working copy, make sure it's up-to-date, and use the same merge command to get the fix.

In many cases the simpler method of just tracking the revisions committed during a bug fix will work fine, so use it if you can. Some bug tracking software includes a place to track revision numbers explicitly, but if yours doesn't you can just put revision numbers into the bug's comments field.

8.6 Developer Experimental Branches

Sometimes developers need to make wide-ranging changes to a project (for example, to change a persistence layer or introduce a new security mechanism). These kinds of things take a minimum of several days to code, and (unfortunately) they can't be introduced incrementally: they just affect too much code. These changes are typically at a low level in the application and normally have a far-reaching impact on the rest of the system.

If a single developer wants to make a wide-ranging change to the source, they could work in their local workspace. However, this has a couple of potential downsides. First, the developer loses the benefit of version control while they're working on the change; also, they lose the ability to revert just sections of their work, they lose revision history, and so on. They also don't have their work in a central repository, so there's a chance it won't be backed up.

If multiple developers are working on a wide-ranging change, then they have bigger problems; they need to be able to share changes and work on the same (experimental) code base.

The answer is to put the experimental code into a branch in the version control system. The developers working on the changes use that branch in their workspace. When they've finished their work, they can make the decision about integrating their work into the trunk. If they decide that experiment is a failure, they can abandon the branch. Otherwise they simply merge the changes made in the branch into the trunk. Whatever their decision, future work continues in the trunk, and the branch becomes history.

Creating a developer branch is effectively the same as creating a release branch. We copy the trunk into a new experimental branch directory, stored alongside release branches:[3]

```
work> svn copy -m "new hibernate persistence spike" \
             svn://olio/sesame/trunk                \
             svn://olio/sesame/branches/TRY-MGM-hbn-spike
Committed revision 45.
```

To start using the branch, you need to either check it out into a new working copy or switch an existing working copy to the new branch.

---

[3]You might not want experimental branches cluttering up your release branches directory, and Subversion is perfectly happy to let you put a branch anywhere you like. Just make sure you remember that /branches/cb/fluffy contains that new persistence framework you're betting the company on....

8.7 Working with Experimental Code

If you have a working copy of your project already checked out, you can switch it to the new experimental branch using svn switch. Here we'll switch our sesame working copy:

```
work> cd sesame
sesame> svn switch svn://olio/sesame/branches/TRY-MGM-hbn-spike
At revision 45.
```

To switch the sesame working copy back to the trunk, we use svn switch again:

```
sesame> svn switch svn://olio/sesame/trunk
At revision 45.
```

Instead of reusing a working copy, you can check out the branch into a new directory. This is our preferred option, because it's harder to get confused about what you're working on:

```
work> svn co svn://olio/sesame/branches/TRY-MGM-hbn-spike hbn-spike
A   hbn-spike/Month.txt
A   hbn-spike/Number.txt
A   hbn-spike/common
A   hbn-spike/common/Log.java
A   hbn-spike/common/Clock.java
A   hbn-spike/Day.txt
A   hbn-spike/Year.txt
A   hbn-spike/contacts
A   hbn-spike/contacts/Contacts.java
Checked out revision 45.
```

8.8 Merging the Experimental Branch

Once you're happy with the changes you've made in an experimental branch, you'll need to merge them back to the trunk. To do this, first make sure all the developers have checked in their changes and that you have an up-to-date working copy of the trunk (this little dance is the reason we suggest checking out the experimental branch in a different directory).

We need to tell Subversion to merge all the changes in the experimental branch, from when it was created to its latest state, into the trunk. For this, we need to know when the branch was created. Fortunately, svn log has a --stop-on-copy option that will tell us exactly:

```
work> svn log --stop-on-copy   \
        svn://olio/sesame/branches/TRY-MGM-hbn-spike
```

```
------------------------------------------------------------
r47 | mike | 2004-11-12 13:47:13 -0700 (Fri, 12 Nov 2004)
Added hibernate utils
------------------------------------------------------------
r46 | mike | 2004-11-12 13:46:27 -0700 (Fri, 12 Nov 2004)
Made Contacts a hibernate mapped class
------------------------------------------------------------
r45 | mike | 2004-11-12 12:55:21 -0700 (Fri, 12 Nov 2004)
new hibernate persistence spike
------------------------------------------------------------
```

This tells us the TRY-MGM-hbn-spike branch was created at revision 45 (Subversion also told us this when we created the branch, but we might have forgotten by the time we want to merge). Now we can merge all the changes between revision 45 and HEAD into our trunk working copy:

```
work> cd sesame
sesame> svn update
At revision 47.
sesame> svn merge -r 45:HEAD    \
          svn://olio/sesame/branches/TRY-MGM-hbn-spike
A  common/HibernateHelper.java
A  contacts/Contacts.hbn.xml
U  contacts/Contacts.java
```

Now we resolve any conflicts produced during the merge, run our unit tests to make sure everything works, and check in:

```
sesame> # .. run unit tests to make sure everything's ok .. #
sesame> svn commit -m "Merged TRY-MGM-hbn-spike to the trunk"
Adding         common/HibernateHelper.java
Adding         contacts/Contacts.hbn.xml
Sending        contacts/Contacts.java
Transmitting file data .
Committed revision 48.
```

Chapter 9

Creating a Project

The word *project* is fairly loosely defined. One person working for a week to implement a web form can be a project, as can many hundred laboring for many years. But most projects share a set of common characteristics:

- Each project has a name. This may sound trivial, but we tend to give things names when we want to identify them as independent entities. Names don't have to be external brands, approved by marketing and subject to field tests in major metropolitan areas. Project names are simply internal to your organization.

- Each project is cohesive; the components of the project work together to achieve some business aim.

- The components within a project tend to be maintained as a unit; you'll release a version of the project as a whole.

- The stuff in a project shares a common set of engineering standards and guidelines and uses a common architecture.

It is important to consider this list when putting projects into a version control system, as it's often hard to know where to draw the boundaries between different projects. Getting the project structure wrong is a major source of frustration when using version control and can lead to a lot of wasted effort as time goes on. Subversion *does* make it straightforward to move things around once a project has started, but this requires coordination with everyone using the repository.

Subversion organizes everything by directory, so projects will correspond to directory locations inside your repository. Sub-projects might correspond to subdirectories, and so on. This scheme gives you the flexibility to dream up a directory structure that works for your projects, but it can also be a little hard to know where to start.

So, before creating projects in your repository, spend some time planning. For example, is your project going to implement a framework that the company will use in future development efforts? If so, then perhaps that framework should be a separate project in its own right, with your current project and those other future projects sharing in its use. Is your project developing multiple independent components? Perhaps each should be its own project. Or is your project writing an extension for an existing chunk of code? Perhaps then it should be a subproject of that original project.

9.1 Creating the Initial Project

There are basically three ways to create directories (and thus projects) within a Subversion repository:

- Import existing source into a directory in the repository.

- Manually create directories using svn mkdir until you have the desired project structure.

- Convert an existing source code repository. There are Subversion tools to convert CVS, RCS, Visual Source-Safe, and Perforce repositories.

Converting from some other version control system is a big topic and is covered in detail in Appendix B on page 169. That leaves us with two options: import and manual directory creation.

Importing Into Subversion

If you have existing source files (even if it's just the project's README file), you can use the svn import command to pull those files into your repository. In the examples that follow, we'll assume you're working on the Wibble project (the Wickedly Integrated Business-to-Business Lease Exchange).

You'll need a directory tree containing the files you want to import (and only the files you want to import; be sure to clean up all the various backup files and other dross before going any further). Make sure you're in the top-level directory of this tree (in our case, in the directory wibble), and then issue an svn import command:

```
wibble> svn import -m "Wibble initial import"   \
        svn://olio/wibble/trunk
Adding          wibble.build
Adding          src
Adding          src/Wibble.cs
Adding          src/WibbleTest.cs
Adding          README
Committed revision 49.
```

This tells Subversion to import the contents of the current directory, storing it in the repository in /wibble/trunk. Subversion automatically creates parent directories as needed during an import, but you will probably also want the tags and branches directories for your project:

```
wibble> svn mkdir -m "Create tags directory"     \
        svn://olio/wibble/tags
Committed revision 50.
wibble> svn mkdir -m "Create branches directory"  \
        svn://olio/wibble/branches
Committed revision 51.
```

Your project is now checked in. You should check it out using svn checkout, and, if everything is okay, you can delete the original directory tree you used for the import.

Manually Creating Directories

If you don't already have files for your project, an easy way to get started is to create a skeletal directory structure and then flesh things out by adding files.

We can use the svn mkdir command to create directories in the repository. For a Java project, you might want something like Figure 9.1 on the following page. Helpfully, svn mkdir allows you to create multiple directories with a single command.

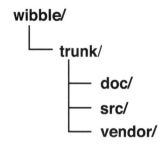

Figure 9.1: WIBBLE PROJECT LAYOUT

```
work> svn mkdir -m "Creating initial structure"    \
      svn://olio/wibble                              \
      svn://olio/wibble/trunk                        \
      svn://olio/wibble/trunk/src                    \
      svn://olio/wibble/trunk/doc                    \
      svn://olio/wibble/trunk/vendor
Committed revision 54.
```

The Wibble project is now ready to check out into a local working copy. You'll be able to add source code, documentation, and libraries in the same way you'd add files during regular development, using the svn add command.

9.2 Structure within the Project

Your company may well already have standards that dictate how to organize the source code and directories within your projects. If you're developing with Java, for example, you might be using the Jakarta conventions for laying out directories.[1] If you don't currently use a standard, what follows are some basic suggestions.

---

[1]http://jakarta.apache.org/site/dirlayout.html

Top-Level Files

These are the typical files you'll find at the top-level of each project:

READDME

> Incredible though it seems, a couple of years from now
> the latest red-hot project will have faded down to a dull
> gray, and you'll have a hard time remembering exactly
> *what* the Wibble project was all about. So create a file
> called README in the top-level project directory. Write
> a small paragraph describing the project: the business
> problems it is solving, the basic technologies used, and
> so on. This isn't meant to be a full description; it's just
> an *aide-memoir* intended to trigger those long-dormant
> neurons when you come back after a long absence.

BUILDING

> Create another top-level file called BUILDING, containing
> simple hints to future code archaeologists who have the
> unenviable task of rebuilding this project from source.
> Because you'll be automating the build, this document
> will be short; Figure 9.2 on the next page shows an
> example.

GLOSSARY

> Create one more top-level file called GLOSSARY. Make it a
> habit to document all project-specific jargon in this file.
> Not only will this make it easier for future developers
> when they're trying to work out what a "wibble_channel"
> is, but it will also guide the project team when it comes
> to naming classes, methods, and variables.

Top-Level Directories

Most projects have at least the following top-level directories:

doc/

> Check all project documentation into doc and its sub-
> directories. Don't forget to add memos and e-mails that
> describe decisions reached. It's normal to have directo-
> ries under doc that contain different document types or
> for different phases of the project.

```
Prerequisites:
  * Oracle 9.6i (perhaps later versions but
    that configuration's not tested)
  * GCC 2.96
Building:
  ./configure [--with-oracle=<dir>]
  make
  make test
  make install
More info:
  docs/building.html
```

Figure 9.2: SAMPLE BUILDING FILE

If your project needs external documentation (for example, the description of an algorithm or a third-party file format), consider copying this and storing it under the doc directory tree (copyright permitting, of course). This will make it easier for future maintainers if the external site has since gone away. If you can't copy this material into your project, create a file in doc called BIBLIOGRAPHY and add links and a brief description in it.

data/

Many projects carry along data (for example, information needed to populate lookup tables in the database). Keep this data in a single location (if for no other reason that someone, at sometime, will urgently need to find out why we're charging 127 percent sales tax in Guam).

db/

If your project uses a database, store all the schema-related stuff here. Work hard not to fall into the habit of modifying schemas online. Have your database administrator create SQL scripts for each update—scripts that both update the schema *and* migrate the data. By keeping these in the repository, you'll be able to migrate any version of the database to any other version.

src/

The project's source code should be stored under this directory. You might want subdirectories to separate different types of source code, for example, src/java and src/eiffel.

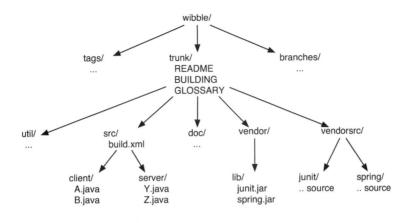

Figure 9.3: WIBBLE PROJECT LAYOUT

util/

A directory to hold various project-specific utility programs, tools, and scripts. Some teams have a directory called tools instead.

vendor/

If your project uses third-party libraries or header files that you want to archive along with your own code, do it under a top-level vendor directory.

vendorsrc/

Sometimes a project will import and include code from a third party (for example, if it is using an open-source library and needs to ensure that it will have access to a particular version of the source for the life of the application). You'll include the binary libraries (and possibly the header files) in the vendor directory, but you'll also want to retain the source from which these libraries were built. Store these sources under the vendorsrc directory. We have more to say about vendor source code in Chapter 10, *Third-Party Code*, on page 137.

A possible file layout for the Wibble project is shown in Figure 9.3. In this project we have our own source code (divided into client and server components) along with some imported open-source code (the JUnit and Spring frameworks).

In addition, many projects will have a standard set of directories that are used during the build or release of the project. These directories do not contain files that should be stored in the repository (as their contents are generated on the fly), but some teams still find it convenient to have these directories appear in every developer's workspace. To do this, you can add these empty directories to the repository; they'll appear in the working copy when developers check out. An equally valid alternative is not to store these directories in Subversion. Instead, have your build scripts create them as needed, and then tidy them up when you're done with them. If you use this scheme, you can add the directory names to the svn:ignore property on your project's top-level directory to stop Subversion cluttering your screen with question marks.

You'll also want to keep your test code somewhere, but opinions vary wildly on where this should be. Some teams like keeping it in parallel directories to their source tree; others put the tests in subdirectories of the source files being tested. To some extent the "correct" answer depends on the language being used. For example, the Java package naming rules mean that if you want to test protected methods you'll need to construct parallel trees (or put your tests in the same directory as the source being tested). We cover this in more detail in the companion book *Pragmatic Unit Testing* [HT03].

There are no hard-and-fast rules for structuring directories in a project. However, being consistent across projects will greatly help people who come along in future and will give you the flexibility to move between projects without experiencing that "I'm totally lost" feeling.

9.3 Sharing Code between Projects

Projects rarely exist in a vacuum, instead being surrounded by other work in an organization. Once a set of projects begins to mature, you'll often find that there are common areas of functionality that could be reused across projects. In a large enterprise it's common to have teams specifically working on reusable frameworks and libraries.

The Subversion "everything is a directory" approach means that your common code will need to live in a shared directory

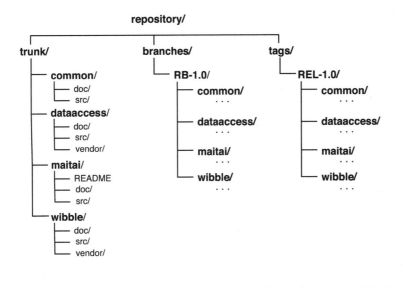

Figure 9.4: REPOSITORY LAYOUT WITH AN ÜBER-PROJECT

in the repository. There are two main ways to accomplish this:

- Store all your projects in a single "über-project" and use a build script to manage dependencies between projects.

- Use svn:externals to pull the dependencies for each project into your working copy before you build.

Both approaches can work, but using svn:externals is more flexible with respect to project organization and branching.

Code Sharing with an Über-project

The repository directory structure when using an über-project is shown in Figure 9.4.

Directly beneath the trunk/ directory are directories for each of the shared projects, in this case common and dataaccess. The directories maitai and wibble store the actual project code for the MaiTai and Wibble projects.

A developer would check out this über-project into a single working copy containing all the projects. What to call this working copy requires creativity and inspiration, neither of which come cheap, so we'll go with uber-project:

```
work> svn checkout svn://olio/trunk/ uber-project
A  uber-project/wibble
A  uber-project/wibble/doc
A  uber-project/wibble/doc/UserRequirements.doc
A  uber-project/wibble/src
A  uber-project/wibble/src/WibbleTest.java
    :         :              :
A  uber-project/dataaccess/lib/neo-1.3.0.dll
A  uber-project/dataaccess/src
A  uber-project/dataaccess/src/DataMapper.cs
A  uber-project/dataaccess/README
Checked out revision 17.
```

When a developer comes to build the MaiTai project, they'd (quite rightly) expect the build script to first build the projects on which MaiTai depends. In this case it might first build the data access project. Once all the dependencies are built—and assuming the data access project produces a library as part of its build—the MaiTai project can use that library and build happily.

This strategy has a couple of drawbacks. First, developers have to check out *all* the code for *all* the projects in your repository. This might not be desirable if you have a large repository or if some of the source is sensitive and requires stricter access controls. Second, the branching options are limited—you pretty much have to branch all the code at once, rather than on a project-by-project basis.

Code Sharing with Externals

A special Subversion directory property, svn:externals, lets you include the contents of another repository in your working copy. Subversion properties and how to manipulate them are covered more fully in Section 6.4, *Properties*, on page 67.

The svn:externals property is set on a directory and specifies a list of repository URLs to include when checking out. You can use any Subversion repository you like in an externals definition—the client will do the work of checking out for you. This means that it is possible to include code from Subversion repositories that aren't under your direct control, for example, open-source projects hosted on the internet.

Figure 9.5 on the facing page and Figure 9.6 on page 134 show views of a repository that uses externals to link shared

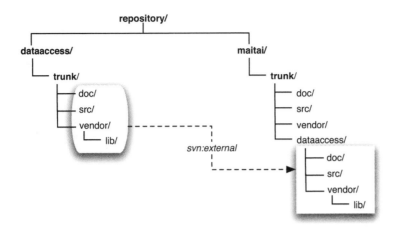

Figure 9.5: REPOSITORY LAYOUT USING EXTERNALS

code into particular projects. There's a lot going on here, so we'll cover it piece by piece.

Let's look at the MaiTai project first. It is stored in /maitai/trunk (shown in Figure 9.5). This has a dependency on the data access project, in particular on /dataaccess/trunk. The filenames in boxes show where these files are imported to the MaiTai tree using externals. In order to set up the dependency, we check out a working copy of the MaiTai project and set the svn:externals property:

```
work> svn checkout svn://olio/maitai/trunk maitai
A   maitai/lib
A   maitai/src
Checked out revision 19.
work> svn propset svn:externals                    \
         "dataaccess svn://olio/dataaccess/trunk"  \
         maitai
property 'svn:externals' set on 'maitai'
```

Here we've set the svn:externals property to include just a single external. You can use svn propedit to bring up an editor if you have multiple dependencies, which should each be listed on a different line.

The externals definition has two parts: first we name the directory inside the MaiTai project where Subversion should

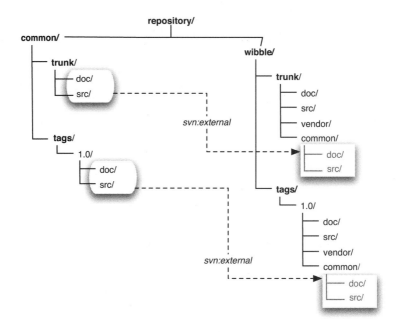

Figure 9.6: REPOSITORY LAYOUT USING EXTERNALS

---

include /dataaccess/trunk, and then we provide the repository URL we'd like to include. Performing an update on the working copy will cause the Subversion client to pull in the data access project:

```
work> cd maitai
maitai> svn update
Fetching external item into 'dataaccess'
A  dataaccess/lib
A  dataaccess/src
Updated external to revision 19.

Updated to revision 19.
```

We still need to commit the property change on the maitai directory to let other developers see this new external item.

```
maitai> svn commit -m "Added dataaccess project as an external"
Sending        .
Committed revision 20.
```

Externals provide much more flexibility when working with branches. Figure 9.6 shows that the Wibble project depends on common. Furthermore, the trunk of Wibble depends on the trunk of common, but the 1.0 branch of Wibble depends on the 1.0 branch of common. We can do this by changing the svn:externals definition for the Wibble project after we branch it. Externals also allow you to be very precise about the dependencies each project has—developers don't have to check out every piece of code in the repository in order to start working.

An important point to note is that Subversion will *not* automatically commit changes you make to a checked-out external when you commit changes to the project that included it. You need to explicitly commit changes to each external by changing to the directory in which it's included and running svn commit.

We recommend treating dependencies as "read-only" in each project—if a developer working on MaiTai needs to fix a bug in the data access project, he should check out /dataaccess/trunk, fix the bug, check in, and then do an update in his MaiTai working copy to get the fix.

Chapter 10

Third-Party Code

All projects rely to some extent on external libraries: Java programs use rt.jar, .NET programs use mscorlib.dll, and so on. Should these libraries form part of your working copy when you check out from the repository?

To answer that question, ask yourself another. You need to be able to rebuild a working program at some arbitrary time in the future. Will you be able to use the versions of these libraries that will be available then?

10.1 Binary Libraries

If you feel comfortable that the libraries used by your code will be available (and compatible) over the life of your application, then there's no need to do anything special with them; just use them as installed on your machine.

Looking beyond standard language facilities, many projects include other, less stable libraries in their projects. For example, many .NET developers will use the NUnit[1] framework to test their code. Compared to the standard libraries, these frameworks are fairly volatile (as of November 2004, NUnit is up to version 2.2). Although the changes between versions are mostly compatible, changes can affect your application. As a result, we recommend you include these libraries in your project's repositories.

---

[1]http://www.nunit.org/

Having made the decision you want to include a third-party library in your workspace and repository, you now have to decide what to include and where to put it.

The first decision is what files to include. This is relatively easy. If you use the library in the form distributed by the maker, and you feel confident that the library will continue to work unmodified through the life of the application, then storing the binary form of the library is all that is needed. We suggest putting all these libraries in subdirectories of a top-level vendor/ directory inside your project.

If the library is architecture independent (for example, a Java .jar file), then it can simply sit in a subdirectory called lib. If the file as packaged by the vendor has a version number in the name, such as junit-3.8.1.jar, we suggest giving it a more generic name. In this case, you'd add junit.jar to your repository. This makes upgrading easy—just copy over a new version of the library and check in. You won't need to change your build scripts or include files. In any case, you should state the version number of the library in your commit message so later you can figure out what version you're using.

If instead you have libraries that depend on the target architecture (assuming your application is targeted at more than one architecture), you'll need to have subdirectories below vendor for each architecture and operating system combination. A common naming scheme for these subdirectories is to use arch-os where arch is the target architecture (i586 for an Intel Pentium, ppc for a PowerPC, and so on) and os is the operating system (linux, win2k, osx, and so on).

Languages such as C and C++ require that you include source header files in application code that uses a particular library. These header files are supplied with the library and should also be stored in the repository. We suggest storing them in an include subdirectory beneath vendor. Structure the directories beneath vendor/include in such a way that the compilers can find the libraries' include files naturally. As an example, consider a C library called *datetime*, which performs date and time calculations. It comes with a binary library archive, lib-datetime.a, and two header files, datetime.h and extras.h. The datetime.h header library is intended to be installed at the top

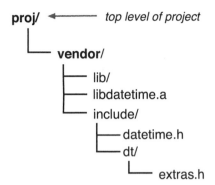

Figure 10.1: SAMPLE REPOSITORY WITH THIRD-PARTY LIBRARY

level of the include hierarchy, extras.h is expected to be in a subdirectory called dt. That is, a program that used both header files would normally start like this:

```
#include <datetime>
#include <dt/extras>
// . . .
```

In this case, we'd organize our repository (and our working copy) as shown in Figure 10.1.

Integrating with the Build Environment

If you include vendor libraries or header files in your repository, you'll need to make sure your compilers, linkers, and IDEs can get to them. There's a minor problem: you need to make sure you don't check anything into the repository that contains absolute path names (as this might not work on some other developer's machine). Instead, you have a couple of options:

- Arrange your build tools so that all path names are relative to (say) the top-level project directory. This is workable if you're using an external build tool such as make or ant, but it can get tricky.

- Set up some external environment variable to point to the top of the project tree, and make all references in the build relative to this variable. This allows each developer to have different values in the external variable but then to share a common build environment layout.

The external variable need not be a true operating system environment variable. The Eclipse IDE, for example, allows each user to set internal variables and then to have a common shared build structure that references these variables. This means all developers can share a common Eclipse build definition but that developers can still install the source in different locations.

We recommend the second approach.

10.2   Libraries with Source Code

Sometimes a library comes with source code (or is distributed only as source code). If you have both source and binary versions of the library available, which should you store in the repository, and how should you set up your working copy?

The answer is an exercise in risk management. Having the source available means you are always in the position (technically, at least) to fix bugs and add features, something you can't do with a binary library. This is clearly a good thing. At the same time, including the source code for all the libraries used by your project can slow down builds and complicate the structure of your project. It also gives future maintainers a headache. If there's a bug, do they need to consider potential changes to the library source, or can they concentrate on the code written by your organization?

Our recommendation is to add vendor source to your repository, but to treat it specially. To do this you have to do a bit of role playing.

Imagine for a minute that you are the writer of this particular library and that every now and then you release an updated version of the code to your user base. Being a high-quality library writer, you naturally put all your source in a version control system and practice all the necessary release control procedures.

Now come back from the role play (remember, breathe in, breathe out, breathe in, breathe out). In an ideal world, we should be able to hook straight into our vendor's repository and extract releases directly from there. But we can't, so we have to do the work ourselves. Whenever we receive code, bug fixes, and new releases from a vendor, we have to pretend that *we* generated the code and handle it in our version control system as if we were the vendor handling it in theirs.

Importing Vendor Source for the First Time

When we first receive the source code for a third-party library, we need to import it into our repository. Vendor code is stored on a *vendor branch*, and each time we receive code and import it it's called a *vendor drop*. We recommend keeping vendor branches separate from the code of your project. If you anticipate importing code from multiple sources over time, it probably makes sense to keep it all under a common top-level directory; we suggest calling it /vendorsrc.

vendor branch

vendor drop

Each library or product you want to track will live in its own vendor branch beneath /vendorsrc, such as /vendorsrc/sun/jdbc. Within the vendor branch directory we'll have a current directory storing the most recent vendor drop (kind of like the trunk directory for a regular project). Alongside this we'll have directories containing tags for each vendor drop.

To make this more concrete, let's assume we've decided to use version 1.0.0 of the jMock[2] mock objects library (after checking the license terms, of course).

Start by downloading the latest release from the jMock web site. Save jmock-1.0.0-src.jar to a temporary directory, and then use WinZip (or plain old jar) to extract the contents. This should leave you with a folder called jmock-1.0.0 containing all the jMock source code, documentation, and examples.

Now we can import the drop into the repository. We'll store it under /vendorsrc/codehaus/jmock/current. In this case, the vendor is CodeHaus, and the "product" is jMock. Run svn import from the directory above jmock-1.0.0:

[2]http://jmock.codehaus.org/

```
tmp> svn import --no-autoprops -m "Import jMock 1.0.0"  \
        jmock-1.0.0                                      \
        svn://olio/vendorsrc/codehaus/jmock/current
Adding          jmock-1.0.0/extensions
Adding          jmock-1.0.0/extensions/cglib
Adding          jmock-1.0.0/extensions/cglib/acceptance-tests
Adding          jmock-1.0.0/extensions/cglib/acceptance-tests/atest
Adding          jmock-1.0.0/extensions/cglib/acceptance-tests/atest/jmock
       :    :        :    :
Adding  (bin)   jmock-1.0.0/examples/classes/.../Calculator.class
Adding  (bin)   jmock-1.0.0/examples/classes/.../ParseException.class
Adding  (bin)   jmock-1.0.0/examples/classes/.../InfixParser.class
Committed revision 3.
```

Next, tag the vendor drop, marking it as version 1.0.0. If CodeHaus releases a new version of jMock, you'll be able track the two versions effectively:

```
tmp> svn copy -m "Tag 1.0.0 vendor drop"                        \
        svn://olio/vendorsrc/codehaus/jmock/current             \
        svn://olio/vendorsrc/codehaus/jmock/1.0.0
Committed revision 4.
```

Updating to a New Vendor Release

When jMock 1.0.1 comes along, we'd like to be able to incorporate it into our repository. To do this, think back to our role play—we are pretending to be CodeHaus, maintaining our code in /vendorsrc/codehaus/jmock/current. When we released 1.0.0, we tagged the code by copying it to jmock/1.0.0. We continue to develop our code, working on our "trunk." Once we reach our next release, we make another tag to mark 1.0.1.

Outside of the role play, we don't actually get to see any of the changes that are made to the jMock code. We see only the result, jmock-1.0.1-src.jar. In order to emulate what's going on in the jMock repository, we need to update the contents of *our* directory /vendorsrc/codehaus/jmock/current so that it looks like the new release. We update our copy of the jMock code so that it looks like *we* did all the work to get us to 1.0.1.

How do we get our copy to look like the new release? Well, since the last release CodeHaus will have modified some files, added some new files, maybe moved a few files around, and occasionally deleted files. We need to perform all these operations in current.

Whilst this synchronization could be done by hand, it's all pretty labor intensive and prone to mistakes. Fortunately, Subversion has a utility to import new vendor drops automatically, performing the adds and deletes for you. The magic is provided by a Perl script called svn_load_dirs.pl.[3]

The script requires Perl to be installed on your system, along with a few modules (such as the URI module for manipulating URLs). When run, it requires three arguments:

Base URL

> The base URL of the Subversion repository to work with. It expects to find all the drops for a particular product beneath this directory. In our example so far, this would be svn://olio/vendorsrc/codehaus/jmock.

"Current" Directory

> The directory beneath the base URL in which the latest vendor drop can be found. We're using current in this example.

Directory to Import

> The directory on the local machine from which to import the new vendor drop.

You can also specify a -t tagname option to automatically tag the new vendor drop.

Download the new release of jMock, storing it in jmock-1.0.1 in your temporary directory. Now run svn_load_dirs.pl to load the new release and tag it:

```
tmp> svn_load_dirs.pl -t 1.0.1                       \
       svn://olio/vendorsrc/codehaus/jmock current jmock-1.0.1
Directory jmock-1.0.1 will be tagged as 1.0.1
Please examine identified tags.  Are they acceptable? (Y/n) y
```

We're being asked if tagging the new source from jmock-1.0.1 as "1.0.1" is okay. That's what we want to do, so type y and hit Enter. The rest of the process is hands free:

```
Checking that the base URL is a Subversion repository.
Running /usr/local/bin/svn log -r HEAD svn://olio/vendorsrc/codehaus/jmock
Finding the root URL of the Subversion repository.
Running /usr/local/bin/svn log -r HEAD svn://olio
Determined that the svn root URL is svn://olio.
```

---

[3]http://svn.collab.net/repos/svn/trunk/contrib/client-side

```
Native EOL on this system is \012.

Finding if any directories need to be created in repository.
Running /usr/local/bin/svn log -r HEAD svn://olio/.../jmock/current
No directories need to be created to prepare repository.
Checking out svn://olio/.../jmock/current into /tmp/...
Running /usr/local/bin/svn checkout svn://olio/.../jmock/current my_import_wc

Loading jmock-1.0.1 and will save in tag 1.0.1.
U    build.properties
U    VERSION
U    CHANGELOG
U    core/src/test/jmock/core/InvocationTest.java
U    core/src/test/jmock/core/testsupport/MockInvocationMatcher.java
U    core/src/test/jmock/core/matcher/InvokedRecorderTest.java
U    core/src/org/jmock/core/matcher/InvokeAtLeastOnceMatcher.java
     :           :               :
Running /usr/local/bin/svn propget svn:eol-style VERSION
Running /usr/local/bin/svn propget svn:eol-style CHANGELOG
     :           :               :
Running /usr/local/bin/svn commit --file /tmp/svn_load_...
Running /usr/local/bin/svn update
     :           :               :
Cleaning up /tmp/svn_load_dirs_ZH6k9TLxFM
```

Examining the Subversion log, we can see that the changes between jMock 1.0.0 and 1.0.1 have been applied to our copy of the code:

```
tmp> svn log -v svn://olio/vendorsrc/codehaus/jmock/current
------------------------------------------------------------
r5 | mike | 2004-11-18 17:03:06 -0700 (Thu, 18 Nov 2004)
Changed paths:
   M /vendorsrc/codehaus/jmock/current/CHANGELOG
   M /vendorsrc/codehaus/jmock/current/VERSION
   M /vendorsrc/codehaus/jmock/current/build.properties
     :           :               :
Load jmock-1.0.1 into vendorsrc/codehaus/jmock/current.
------------------------------------------------------------
```

We can follow the same process to import new releases of jMock, as they become available.

Using Vendor Code in a Project

All this fancy importing is great so far—you've got your own copy of the jMock source code and have tagged it for posterity. Now we need to actually use that source in a project. To do this, copy the vendor branch into your project, storing it in vendor/jmock:

```
work> svn mkdir -m "" svn://olio/maitai/trunk/vendor
work> svn copy -m "MaiTai needs jMock"                         \
             svn://olio/vendorsrc/codehaus/jmock/1.0.0    \
             svn://olio/maitai/trunk/vendor/jmock
Committed revision 12.
```

When we check out MaiTai, we'll get a copy of the jMock code:

```
work> svn checkout svn://olio/maitai/trunk maitai
A  maitai/doc
A  maitai/src
A  maitai/vendor
A  maitai/vendor/jmock
A  maitai/vendor/jmock/extensions
       :    :    :    :
A  maitai/vendor/jmock/build.xml
Checked out revision 12.
```

Modifying Vendor Code

Now that you have the vendor's source code, you're free to make modifications to it, safe in the knowledge that you'll be able to easily incorporate new releases whilst preserving your custom changes.

Let's say we want to make some tweaks to jMock's exception handling and expectation framework. Make your changes within the MaiTai working copy, and commit them as normal:

```
maitai> svn status
M       vendor/jmock/core/src/org/jmock/expectation/ExpectationList.java
M       vendor/jmock/core/src/org/jmock/util/NotImplementedException.java
maitai> svn commit -m "Made some custom changes to jMock"
Sending  vendor/jmock/core/src/org/jmock/expectation/ExpectationList.java
Sending  vendor/jmock/core/src/org/jmock/util/NotImplementedException.java
Transmitting file data ..
Committed revision 13.
```

Subversion tracks the change you've made just like regular changes to code you authored yourself.

Updating Modified Code

Life is good. The MaiTai project is doing well and is a success for your company. The guys at CodeHaus release a new version of jMock, and you'd like to incorporate that into the MaiTai project. After loading and tagging the new vendor drop, you're ready to upgrade MaiTai.

We need to merge the changes made to jMock between 1.0.0 and 1.0.1. To do this, use the svn merge command:

```
maitai> svn merge svn://olio/vendorsrc/codehaus/jmock/1.0.0   \
                  svn://olio/vendorsrc/codehaus/jmock/1.0.1   \
                  vendor/jmock
U  vendor/jmock/VERSION
U  vendor/jmock/CHANGELOG
      :    :    :
U  vendor/jmock/build.properties
```

Subversion applies the changes to your working copy. If any conflicts arise between your custom modifications and the 1.0.1 changes, you'll need to fix them as you would a conflict between two developers. Once any conflicts are resolved, and you've run the tests to make sure everything's still working, commit the changes to the repository:

```
maitai> svn commit -m "Updated MaiTai with jMock 1.0.1"
Sending        vendor/jmock/CHANGELOG
Sending        vendor/jmock/VERSION
Sending        vendor/jmock/build.properties
               :      :      :
Transmitting file data ....................
Committed revision 14.
```

10.3 Keyword Expansion during Imports

In these examples, we're importing third-party code (probably from a version control system other than Subversion) into our repository. If we're importing code from CVS, for example, the authors may have included $Author$ or Id keywords. We discussed keywords more fully in Section 6.4, *Keyword Expansion*, on page 69.

The problem is that the keywords are expanded every time the file is checked out. If the vendor has used these tags, then the source you receive will have the vendor's information in these fields. However, if you just import these files as they stand and check them back out, Subversion will update the tags, and suddenly your name will appear in the author field. While this may be vaguely satisfying, it will cause problems later when you come to merge in changes with the next vendor release. Subversion will notice that these tag lines have changed, and you'll get conflicts when merging with the vendor's code.

Fortunately, keyword expansion isn't switched on for new files by default. However, if you've enabled autoprops as described in Section 6.4, *Automatic Property Setting*, on page 75, and are setting svn:keywords automatically, keywords expansion might occur. Use the --no-autoprops switch when importing to disable any potential keyword expansion.

Install, Network, Secure, and Administer Subversion

Subversion client installation is pretty straightforward, often just requiring the right download for your operating system. Running a server is a little more complicated, and many people, especially those migrating from CVS, will want to run a Subversion server on a Unix platform. Subversion's database backend also requires a different backup strategy than a plain file-based version control system. This chapter includes Windows and Linux instructions for installing Subversion, getting your repository on the network, and backing it up in case the worst should happen. There's also a discussion on securing your repository so prying eyes can't get at your data.

A.1 Installing Subversion

Subversion comes packaged for a variety of operating systems.[1] If you're using a Unix-based system, Subversion might be available as an official package, so check first using your package manager.

Windows Installation

The friendly Windows installer makes short work of installing Subversion, even putting the binaries in your path. If you're

---

[1]Go to http://subversion.tigris.org/project_packages.html for the full set of packages.

planning on installing Apache as well, install it *before* Subversion. That way, the Subversion installer will automatically copy Subversion's Apache modules to the right places.

Linux Installation

Here we'll cover installation on Fedora Core 3, which happens to include Subversion 1.1 as a standard package. You can either use the Fedora Package Manager to install the packages or download them by hand.

Visit the Fedora site,[2] and download the following RPMs (don't worry if the version numbers are different; just get the latest releases): subversion-1.1.0-5.i386.rpm, swig-1.3.21-6.i386.rpm, and neon-0.24.7-4.i386.rpm.

Installation is pretty simple. Just change to the directory where you downloaded the RPMs, and run

```
rpms> rpm -hvi subversion-1.1.0-5.i386.rpm \
              swig-1.3.21-6.i386.rpm        \
              neon-0.24.7-4.i386.rpm
Preparing...            ######################### [100%]
   1:neon                ######################### [ 33%]
   2:swig                ######################### [ 67%]
   3:subversion          ######################### [100%]
```

Subversion is now installed and ready to go.

A.2   Networking with svnserve

svnserve is a simple network server for Subversion. It's fast and lightweight, and it's suitable for use on a corporate LAN where traffic is safe from eavesdroppers.

svnserve on Windows

To start svnserve on Windows, go to your command prompt and type

```
C:\> start svnserve --daemon --root c:\svn-repos
```

A new window will pop open with the title svnserve.exe. If you're using Windows XP or have other firewalling software installed, you may be asked whether the server should be

---

[2]http://download.fedora.redhat.com/pub/fedora/linux/core/3/i386/os/Fedora/RPMS/

allowed to accept network connections, in which case choose to unblock svnserve. We've asked svnserve to start in daemon mode with the --daemon option (Windows doesn't actually run it as a daemon; this option is a quirk needed to get svnserve to start), and we're allowing access to the repository named with the --root argument.

Popping open a new window isn't great, since you might close it accidentally. You can add a /B just after the start command if you want svnserve to run without its own window, but in this case you'll need to use Task Manager to kill it off when you're done.

If you'd like svnserve to run whenever your Windows server boots, you'll need to install it as a service. Magnus Norddahl maintains a simple service wrapper called svnservice, available from `http://dark.clansoft.dk/~mbn/svnservice/`.

svnserve on Unix

Starting svnserve is very similar on Unix:

```
home> svnserve --daemon --root /home/mike/svn-repos
```

Your command prompt returns immediately leaving svnserve running as a daemon. Running ps should show the process still running.

Try accessing the repository from a different machine on your network. The example server for this book is called olio, so you'd run

```
work> svn co svn://olio/sesame/trunk vizier
A  vizier/Number.txt
A  vizier/Day.txt
Checked out revision 7.
```

If this doesn't work, you might need to check if there's a firewall between the two machines. If there is (for example, ZoneAlarm, Windows XP's built-in firewall, or a Unix firewall), you'll need to make sure the machine running svnserve can accept connections on TCP port 3690.

Once set up, you should secure your repository, because by default svnserve allows read-only anonymous access to everything. Refer to Section A.5, *svnserve*, on page 159 for more details.

A.3 Networking with svn+ssh

Windows doesn't usually support incoming SSH connections, so this section covers Unix configuration only. You might be able to get Putty working as a Windows SSH server, but it's definitely not for the faint of heart!

When a user specifies a svn+ssh scheme to access the repository, the Subversion client runs SSH to connect to the server. This means each user needs an account on the server, and the password they're asked for is their Unix account password. If your users have public/private key pairs or are running an SSH agent, Subversion automatically takes advantage of those features.

Subversion tries to run svnserve -t on the server in order to access the repository. If Subversion complains it can't find svnserve, make sure the default path on the server contains the svnserve binary. Because Subversion starts svnserve using the -t (tunnel) option, you don't need to have it running as a daemon like you do with plain svn connections.

Once the SSH connection is established and svnserve is running in tunnel mode, Subversion will attempt to access the repository's files. It does this as the same user who authenticated via SSH, which means all the users of your repository need read and write access to the repository files. Furthermore, any *new* files that are created need to be readable and writable for all the other users.[3]

In order for multiple Unix users to access the repository, they should all be in a single Unix group and have a umask of 002 when running svnserve via SSH. You also need to set the group "sticky bit" on the repository directories. Here's a step-by-step guide to setting this up.

First create a Unix group for everyone using Subversion, and add each user to the group. These commands are Linux specific, so you might need to tweak them a bit for your flavor of Unix:

---

[3]Getting this part wrong is the most common cause for "wedged" repositories. During the commit BDB might decide to create new files that are part of the repository. If these aren't writable by other users their Subversion clients will hang trying to access the repository.

```
root> /usr/sbin/groupadd subversion
root> /usr/sbin/usermod -G subversion mike
root> /usr/sbin/usermod -G subversion ian
```

Next, change the ownership of your repository directory and files to the new group, and set the group sticky bit for the repository db directory:

```
root> chgrp -R subversion /home/svn-repos
root> chmod -R 770 /home/svn-repos
root> chmod g+S /home/svn-repos/db
```

Now try checking out from the repository. Here we'll specify an exact username for the remote machine, and the password we're asked for is our Unix password:

```
work> svn checkout                                        \
          svn+ssh://mike@olio/home/svn-repos/sesame/trunk  \
          sesame
mike@olio's password:
A  sesame/Number.txt
A  sesame/Day.txt
Checked out revision 7.
```

This is all a bit complicated, but well worth it if you'd like to take advantage of SSH for securing your connections. More information is available online.[4]

Troubleshooting an SSH Connection

Connecting to a repository using svn+ssh needs quite a few programs to be working and configured correctly. Unfortunately, Subversion's error messages are sometimes less informative than they could be. Here's a rough guide to things that can go wrong and how to fix them.

svn: The system cannot find the file specified. (Windows)

Subversion is complaining that it can't find "the file specified." In this case it's looking for ssh in order to make a secure connection (the svn command is being found just fine). The usual fix for this is to edit your Subversion configuration as described back in Section 5.1, *svn+ssh*, on page 57 and make sure that plink.exe is available in your path.

---

[4]http://svnbook.red-bean.com/en/1.1/ch06s03.html#
svn-ch-6-sect-3.4

svn: No such file or directory (Unix)

Similar to the Windows "cannot find file specified" problem, Subversion is unable to find the ssh command on your system. This might mean ssh isn't installed on your computer.

Subversion just seems to hang (Windows)

Bring up Task Manager, and see if plink.exe is running. If it's running but Subversion isn't displaying any output, it could be because plink is waiting for user input. This can happen when you connect to an SSH server for the first time and need to accept the server key. Try running plink on its own, saying "yes" when asked to store the key in Putty's cache:

```
work> plink mike@olio.mynetwork.net echo hello
The server's host key is not cached in the registry. You
have no guarantee that the server is the computer you
think it is.
The server's rsa2 key fingerprint is:
ssh-rsa 1024 c3:82:fd:a6:b4:5d:23:f2:1a:f8:8b:04:be:c3
If you trust this host, enter "y" to add the key to
PuTTY's cache and carry on connecting.
  :       :      :
Store key in cache? (y/n) y
mike@olio.mynetwork.net's password:
hello
```

svnserve: command not found

svn: Connection closed unexpectedly

Either or both of these lines is printed by the Subversion client when it can't find svnserve on the server. The SSH connection has been established and you've authenticated as a Unix user, but svnserve isn't in the user's path.

Subversion always attempts to run svnserve -t on the remote server, so unfortunately you can't fix the problem by telling the client where Subversion is installed. You'll need to change the default path on the server, perhaps by editing /etc/profile. Once you've got svnserve in the path, you should be able to test from the client like this:

```
work> ssh mike@olio.mynetwork.net svnserve -t
( success ( 1 2 ( ANONYMOUS EXTERNAL ) ( edit-pipeline ) ) )
```

The `success` message with all the brackets is the start of the svn protocol between the Subversion client and server and means svnserve has been found correctly.

svn: No repository found in 'svn+ssh://myserver/home/svn-repos'

Subversion has successfully connected using SSH and started svnserve. However, svnserve can't find the repository. Check that you're using the correct path to the repository and that you have sufficient permissions to read and create files in the repository directory.

A.4 Networking with Apache

In this section we'll show how to install Apache and configure it to host a Subversion repository. Unix installation instructions vary a bit depending on the exact flavor of Unix, but good instructions are available online. We'll again be using Fedora Core 3 as our example Unix platform.

The Subversion book from the Subversion developers themselves is probably the best complete reference and is available at `http://svnbook.red-bean.com/`

The "How-To" section on the Subversionary web site[5] includes networking instructions for a number of operating systems, including RedHat and Windows.

Apache on Windows

Download and Install Apache

Apache is open-source software, and you can download it for free from `http://httpd.apache.org/download.cgi`.

For a Windows installation, you can download either an .exe or an .msi. The MSI is a Windows Installer package and is a smaller download, so that's probably your best bet. Subversion requires at least Apache 2.0.48—in this example we're using 2.0.50.

---

[5]`http://www.subversionary.org/`

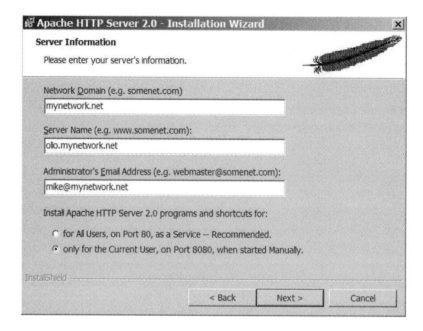

Figure A.1: APACHE SERVER NAME CONFIGURATION

Run the installer, read the first couple of screens including the license agreement and installation notes, and you should get to a screen similar to that in Figure A.1. It's important to get the info on this screen correct, or users might have trouble connecting to Apache. If you're not sure of the settings to use, ask a network administrator to help you.

We'll install Apache for the current user only, on port 8080. Windows machines often already have a web server enabled using the normal HTTP port 80, and we don't want our new Apache server to conflict. If you're setting up a Subversion repository and want to use port 80, make sure Internet Information Services (IIS) has its web server switched off.

At the next step choose Typical Installation, and stick with the default directory for installing Apache. You'll see a few command windows pop open as Apache installs, followed by a message informing you installation was successful.

At the moment, Apache isn't running because we selected the "just for the current user" option when installing. To start

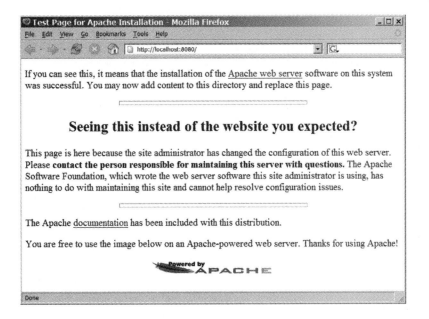

Figure A.2: APACHE TEST PAGE

Apache, choose *Start > All Programs > Apache HTTP Server 2.0.50 > Control Apache Server > Start Apache in Console*. A command prompt window will appear, which means Apache is running.[6] Open a web browser to `http://localhost:8080/`, and you should see a test page like the one in Figure A.2.

Install Subversion's Apache Modules

Subversion integrates with Apache using a number of binary modules that need to be installed in the right places for everything to work properly.

If you're using Windows, open C:\Program Files\Subversion\httpd and copy mod_authz_svn.so and mod_dav_svn.so into the directory C:\Program Files\Apache Group\Apache2\modules. Then go

---

[6]We were going to include a screenshot of the Apache console window, but Dave decided it looked like one of those "Bournemouth by Night" joke postcards, so it got the boot. Don't worry when the Apache window comes up and there's no output—this is how it's supposed to look.

to C:\Program Files\Subversion\bin, and copy the file libdb42.dll into C:\Program Files\Apache Group\Apache2\bin. If you already have Apache installed, the Subversion installer will do this copying for you when you install Subversion.

Configuring Apache

Configuring Apache requires editting .conf files inside your Apache install. The files you need to edit vary a little between systems—Windows uses a single httpd.conf, as do many flavors of Unix, and Red Hat Linux uses a number of smaller files within a conf.d directory.

Choose *Start > All Programs > Apache HTTP Server 2.0.50 > Configure Apache Server > Edit the Apache httpd.conf Configuration file*. This will open Notepad, everyone's favourite editor, with the main Apache configuration file.

Scroll down to the section of the file that reads "Dynamic Shared Object (DSO) Support." You'll see a large number of LoadModule commands, each of which activate extra functionality in Apache. At the bottom of the list, add the following two lines:

```
LoadModule dav_svn_module modules/mod_dav_svn.so
LoadModule authz_svn_module modules/mod_authz_svn.so
```

Next, scroll up a little, and uncomment the existing line for dav_module:

```
LoadModule dav_module modules/mod_dav.so
```

Finally, scroll down to the bottom of the file, and add the following section:

```
<Location /svn-repos>
    DAV svn
    SVNPath c:\svn-repos
</Location>
```

This tells Apache that URLs starting with /svn-repos should use the Subversion DAV module and that the repository is in c:\svn-repos.

If Apache is still running, stop it by closing its command window. Then start Apache by using the Start Apache in Console menu item. Now open your web browser, and hit http://localhost:8080/svn-repos/. If Subversion and

> ## 〵/ Joe Asks...
>
> ### DAV, WebDAV, DeltaV??
>
> As part of its integration with Apache, Subversion uses WebDAV as the protocol between client and server. WebDAV stands for "Web-based Distributed Authoring and Versioning" and is an extension of the HTTP protocol. Instead of rolling their own network protocol, the Subversion developers decided to leverage WebDAV.
>
> Reuse brings a number of advantages, in both speed of development and compatibility with other clients. For example, both Windows and Mac OS X can connect to a WebDAV server and make it available as a network drive.
>
> For further information on WebDAV, including client configuration, see `http://www.webdav.org/`.

Apache are configured correctly, you'll see your repository and the Sesame project, as in Figure A.3 on the next page. Try browsing around the repository—clicking any file will display the latest checked-in version of that file, and clicking a directory will navigate you around.

Apache on Red Hat Linux

Fedora Core 3 comes with Apache installed as standard, so we won't cover that here. You'll need to install the Subversion integration modules and configure Apache to use them.

Install mod_dav_svn

Visit the Fedora site[7] and download the `mod_dav_svn` RPM.[8] Change to the directory where you downloaded the RPM, and run the following command.

---

[7]`http://download.fedora.redhat.com/pub/fedora/linux/core/3/i386/os/Fedora/RPMS/`

[8]Right now, it is `mod_dav_svn-1.1.0-5.i386.rpm`.

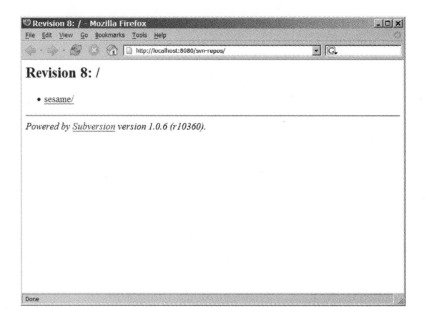

Figure A.3: SUBVERSION REPOSITORY BROWSING

```
rpms> rpm -hvi mod_dav_svn-1.1.0-5.i386.rpm
Preparing...          ######################### [100%]
   1:mod_dav_svn      ######################### [100%]
```

The mod_dav_svn package provides the modules to integrate with Apache and automatically puts them in the right places.

Configure Apache

On Red Hat Linux, Apache uses a number of conf files within /etc/httpd/conf.d. Installing mod_dav_svn adds a new subversion.conf file to that directory, which you'll need to edit to point at your repository. Other flavors of Unix stick with a single httpd.conf file inside /etc/httpd.

The contents of subversion.conf hint at security settings we'll be covering in Section A.5, *Apache Security*, on page 161, but for now just uncomment enough that it points to your repository:

```
<Location /svn-repos>
    DAV svn
    SVNPath /home/svn-repos
</Location>
```

Make sure the svn-repos directory is owned by the Apache user, and reload the Apache configuration files:

```
root> chown -R apache /home/svn-repos
root> /etc/rc.d/init.d/httpd reload
Reloading httpd:                        [  OK  ]
```

At this point your repository is unsecured, allowing read and write access to anonymous users. Don't leave it like this! Section A.5, *Apache Security*, on page 161 details how to secure your Apache hosted repository.

A.5 Securing Subversion

When it comes to accessing a Subversion repository, security lies in two main areas: user authentication and path-based permissions. User authentication is about making sure people connecting to the repository are authorized to do so; it's basically password-protecting your data. Anyone supplying a valid username and password is granted access to the repository. Path-based security goes further, differentiating between users and granting or denying access to individual directories in the repository.

svnserve

By default, svnserve sets up a read-only repository. To get read/write access, we'll need to edit svnserve.conf, which lives inside the svn-repos/conf directory. When you create a repository, svnserve.conf looks something like the one in Figure A.4 on the following page.

If you're familiar with .conf files, you'll see that the entire file is commented out (lines starting with # are comments). Whilst Subversion is trying to be helpful and give us some hints for writing a config file, most people just end up confused by the file. Let's just ignore the defaults and create a simple svnserve.conf:

```
[general]
anon-access = read
auth-access = write
password-db = passwd
```

svnrepos/conf/svnserve.conf

This tells svnserve to allow anonymous read-only access to the repository and to allow read/write access for authenticated

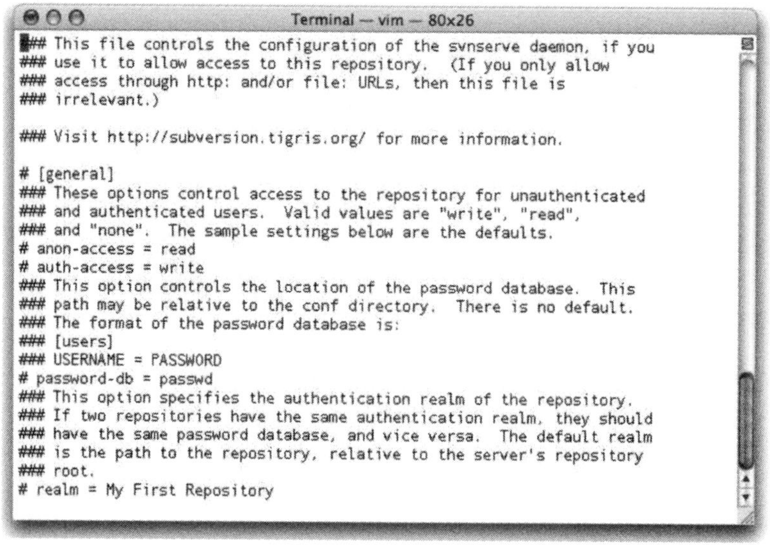

```
Terminal — vim — 80x26
### This file controls the configuration of the svnserve daemon, if you
### use it to allow access to this repository.  (If you only allow
### access through http: and/or file: URLs, then this file is
### irrelevant.)

### Visit http://subversion.tigris.org/ for more information.

# [general]
### These options control access to the repository for unauthenticated
### and authenticated users.  Valid values are "write", "read",
### and "none".  The sample settings below are the defaults.
# anon-access = read
# auth-access = write
### This option controls the location of the password database.  This
### path may be relative to the conf directory.  There is no default.
### The format of the password database is:
### [users]
### USERNAME = PASSWORD
# password-db = passwd
### This option specifies the authentication realm of the repository.
### If two repositories have the same authentication realm, they should
### have the same password database, and vice versa.  The default realm
### is the path to the repository, relative to the server's repository
### root.
# realm = My First Repository
```

Figure A.4: DEFAULTSVNSERVE.CONF

users. We also tell svnserve to look for usernames and passwords in a file called passwd. In the same conf directory, create a password file as follows:

svnrepos/conf/passwd

```
[users]
mike=secret
dave=n1nja123
ian=b4n4n4
```

We've defined three users, each with their own password. In order to commit a change to the repository, a client will have to provide a valid username and password.

svnserve doesn't provide any kind of path-based security, so once a user has read or write access they can get to the whole repository. If you'd like to prevent certain directories from being writable by everyone, you can use a hook script as described in Section A.5, *Access Control with Hook Scripts*, on page 163.

svn+ssh

Connecting to a repository using svn+ssh uses Unix security to determine if a user can access the repository. If they can access the repository's database files they have read/write access to the repository.

As with svnserve, it's possible to use a hook script to achieve path-based security with svn+ssh. It's also possible to host more than one repository on the same Unix server, with different groups of users granted access to each one, using standard Unix permissions.

Apache Security

If you've been following the instructions in this chapter so far, you'll have a repository online using Apache with only a very basic configuration. When set up like this, your repository will have read/write access for everyone, including anonymous users. We'd better fix that up quickly.

Apache provides a wealth of authentication options for users. Here we'll just set up basic password authentication, but you can do fancier stuff including authenticating against a Windows domain. Basic authentication requires a password file with all your usernames and passwords in it, and you need to use the htpasswd utility that comes with Apache to create it.

If you're on Windows, open a command prompt and change to the C:\Program Files\Apache Group\Apache2\bin directory, and then run

```
bin> htpasswd -c -m c:\svn-repos\conf\htpasswd mike
New password: ******
Re-type new password: ******
Adding password for user mike
```

On Unix, htpasswd should be in your path already, so run

```
home> htpasswd -c -m /home/svn-repos/conf/htpasswd mike
New password: ******
Re-type new password: ******
Adding password for user mike
```

Once the file is created, you can add new users to it by dropping the -c flag:

```
bin> htpasswd -m c:\svn-repos\conf\htpasswd dave
New password: ********
Re-type new password: ********
Adding password for user dave
```

Next we need to tell Apache to authenticate users before they are allowed to access the repository. We can do this by requiring a valid user for *all* operations, or just for those folks who actually modify the repository (and thus leave anonymous browsing enabled). To lock things down completely, modify your Apache `Location` directive as follows:

```
<Location /svn-repos>
DAV svn
SVNPath c:\svn-repos

AuthType Basic
AuthName "Subversion Repository"
AuthUserFile c:\svn-repos\conf\htpasswd
Require valid-user
</Location>
```

If instead you'd like anonymous read-only access, configure Apache like this:

```
<Location /svn-repos>
DAV svn
SVNPath c:\svn-repos

AuthType Basic
AuthName "Subversion Repository"
AuthUserFile c:\svn-repos\conf\htpasswd

<LimitExcept GET PROPFIND OPTIONS REPORT>
    Require valid-user
</LimitExcept>
</Location>
```

Your configuration changes will take effect once you restart Apache.

If you have an SSL certificate for your Apache server, you can require a secure connection when accessing the repository. This will encrypt all traffic between the Subversion client and the repository, including passwords and file contents, and is generally a good idea if you're making your repository available over the internet. Edit your Apache configuration once more, and add `SSLRequireSSL`:

```
<Location /svn-repos>
DAV svn
SVNPath c:\svn-repos

AuthType Basic
AuthName "Subversion Repository"
AuthUserFile c:\svn-repos\conf\htpasswd
Require valid-user
SSLRequireSSL
</Location>
```

Apache can be used to set up path-based security, including marking sections of the repository as unreadable for certain users. This is accomplished using mod_authz_svn. See the

Red-Bean Subversion book at `http://svnbook.red-bean.com/en/1.0/ch06s04.html`.

Access Control with Hook Scripts

Subversion can be configured with a number of *hook scripts*   *hook scripts*
that are run on the server at certain times during a commit.
The pre-commit hook runs before a commit is allowed to proceed, and if it returns a nonzero exit status, Subversion dis-
allows the commit.

Pre-commit hooks have access to information about which
files are being changed, as well as the user attempting to
change them. We can use this information to set up path-
based security—if a user attempts to change a file or directory
to which they have not been granted access, our hook script
exits with a one and Subversion stops the commit.

Subversion comes with commit-access-control.pl, which should
get installed somewhere on your machine when you install
Subversion. For Fedora Core 3, for example, it's bundled with
the Subversion documentation in /usr/share/doc.

Copy commit-access-control.pl to the hooks directory in your
repository. Also copy commit-access-control.cfg.example, which
you should rename to ditch the .example extension.

Inside your hooks directory, rename pre-commit.tmpl and make
it executable:

```
hooks> mv pre-commit.tmpl pre-commit
hooks> chmod +x pre-commit
```

The pre-commit template does two things – it checks that the
log message being used contains some text (which you may or
may not be worried about) and then calls the access control
script to check the user's permissions.

Configure the permissions in commit-access-control.cfg, and
you should be ready to go.

Python fans might be interested in svnperms.py, included in the
Subversion distribution, which works in a similar fashion.

A.6 Backing Up Your Repository

Backing up your source code makes a lot of sense—after all, your developers are assuming the repository is a safe place to store all their hard work. Subversion uses either Berkeley DB or the "fsfs" filesystem as the backend for your repository, and these can't be backed up like a regular file. If someone makes a change to the repository during a backup, the repository files may be in an inconsistent state, causing the backup to be invalid.[9]

dumpfile

Subversion provides the svnadmin dump command to extract the contents of a repository into a portable *dumpfile*. A dump-file contains information about each revision in the repository and can be backed up like a regular file. The svnadmin load command takes the contents of a dumpfile and loads it into a repository. This can be used to restore from a backup or to copy a repository to another location.

Full Backups

Depending on how large your repository is, and how often you want to make a backup, you might be able to get away with just doing complete dumps of your repository. The following command creates a complete dump of the repository:

```
mike> svnadmin dump ~/svn-repos > dumpfile.041113
* Dumped revision 0.
* Dumped revision 1.
    :     :     :
* Dumped revision 48.
```

Subversion dumps every revision in the repository to the console, which we then save in dumpfile.041113. The resulting file contains everything the repository contains. A typical dump is highly compressible and ready to back up.

Creating a dumpfile using svnadmin will always produce a consistent snapshot of your repository, even if changes are being committed whilst the dump is created. This means you don't need to shut down access to the repository whilst svnadmin dump is running.

---

[9]Using an "fsfs" repository you're more likely to get a consistent backup, especially if you back up the files in a particular order. See http://svn.collab.net/repos/svn/trunk/notes/fsfs for more details.

To restore from the dumpfile into a new repository, use svnad-min load. First we create a new repository (the old one might not be totally corrupt, so don't delete it), and then load the dumpfile:

```
mike> svnadmin create svn-repos2
mike> svnadmin load svn-repos2 < dumpfile.041113
<<< Started new transaction, based on original revision 1
    * adding path : sesame ... done.
    * adding path : sesame/trunk ... done.
    * adding path : sesame/trunk/Day.txt ... done.
    * adding path : sesame/trunk/Number.txt ... done.
------- Committed revision 1 >>>
    :       :       :
<<< Started new transaction, based on original revision 48
    * adding path : sesame/trunk/common/HibernateHelper.java ...COPIED... done.
    * adding path : sesame/trunk/contacts/Contacts.hbn.xml ...COPIED... done.
    * editing path : sesame/trunk/contacts/Contacts.java ... done.
------- Committed revision 48 >>>
```

Subversion replays each revision from the dumpfile and commits to the repository. Once the load is complete, the repository is ready to go and looks exactly as it did when the dump was created.

Incremental Backups

Doing full backups every day is going to eat disk space pretty fast. Fortunately, svnadmin dump takes an --incremental option, along with --revision specifying a revision range, to produce smaller dump files.

Let's say you already have a dump file containing revisions 1 to 100, but the repository is up to revision 104. You can create an incremental dump file by running

```
work> svnadmin dump --incremental --revision 100:104   \
             /home/svn-repos
```

Combining weekly backups with daily incrementals should give you peace of mind without requiring crazy amounts of disk space. With a bit of scripting, we can create a weekly and daily backup routine that remembers the revision numbers for each backup.

The program that follows is the the weekly backup script. As presented it's a very basic Perl script, but it does demonstrate how to use svnlook youngest to find out what revision your repository is currently on.

```perl
#!/usr/bin/perl -w
#
# Perform a weekly backup of a Subversion repository,
# logging the most-recently-backed-up revision so an
# incremental script can be run other days.
$svn_repos = "/home/mike/svn-repos";
$backups_dir = "/home/mike/svn-backup";
$next_backup_file = "weekly-full-backup." . `date +%Y%m%d`;

$youngest = `svnlook youngest $svn_repos`;
chomp $youngest;

print "Backing up to revision $youngest\n";
`svnadmin dump $svn_repos > $backups_dir/$next_backup_file`;
print "Compressing dump file...\n";
print `gzip -9 $backups_dir/$next_backup_file`;

open(LOG, ">$backups_dir/last_backed_up");
print LOG $youngest;
close LOG;
```

Running this script dumps your repository into a file called weekly-full-backup.yyyymmdd and compresses it using gzip. It also saves the most recent revision to be backed up into a file called last_backed_up:

```
svn-backup> ./weekly-backup.pl
Backing up to revision 638
* Dumped revision 0.
* Dumped revision 1.
* Dumped revision 2.
    :    :    :
* Dumped revision 638.
Compressing dump file...
```

The daily backup script uses the revision number saved by the weekly script to dump just what has changed, rather than the whole repository:

```perl
#!/usr/bin/perl -w
#
# Perform a daily backup of a Subversion repository,
# using the previous most-recently-backed-up revision
# to create just an incremental dump.
$svn_repos = "/home/mike/svn-repos";
$backups_dir = "/home/mike/svn-backup";
$next_backup_file = "daily-incremental-backup." . `date +%Y%m%d`;

open(IN, "$backups_dir/last_backed_up");
$previous_youngest = <IN>;
chomp $previous_youngest;
close IN;

$youngest = `svnlook youngest $svn_repos`;
chomp $youngest;

if($youngest eq $previous_youngest) {
    print "No new revisions to back up.\n";
    exit 0;
}
```

```
# We need to backup from the last backed up revision
# to the latest (youngest) revision in the repository
$first_rev = $previous_youngest + 1;
$last_rev = $youngest;

print "Backing up revisions $first_rev to $last_rev...\n";
$svnadmin_cmd = "svnadmin dump --incremental " .
                "--revision $first_rev:$last_rev " .
                "$svn_repos > $backups_dir/$next_backup_file";
'$svnadmin_cmd';

print "Compressing dump file...\n";
print 'gzip -9 $backups_dir/$next_backup_file';

open(LOG, ">$backups_dir/last_backed_up");
print LOG $last_rev;
close LOG;
```

Running this script after some changes have been made will dump just the new revisions:

```
svn-backup> ./daily-backup.pl
Backing up revisions 639:641
* Dumped revision 639.
* Dumped revision 640.
* Dumped revision 641.
Compressing dump file...
```

The daily incremental backups are much smaller than a full backup but don't contain enough information to restore your repository if disaster strikes. To do a restore, you need to first load your most recent full backup, followed by each daily backup:

```
svn-backup> mkdir newrepos
svn-backup> svnadmin create newrepos
svn-backup> zcat weekly-full-backup.20041129.gz |  \
                svnadmin load newrepos
<<< Started new transaction, based on original revision 1
     * adding path : branches ... done.
     * adding path : tags ... done.
     * adding path : trunk ... done.
          :    :    :    :
svn-backup> zcat daily-incremental-backup.20041130.gz |  \
                svnadmin load newrepos
<<< Started new transaction, based on original revision 639
     * editing path : trunk/ccnet/lib/NetReflector.dll ... done.
------- Committed new rev 639 (loaded from original rev 639) >>>
          :    :    :    :
```

Appendix B

Migrating to Subversion

So you're sold on the benefits of using Subversion. You like its support for atomic commits, its changesets, its speedy network protocols, and its real branching and merging. You've even convinced your boss that Subversion is right for your team. The only minor problem standing between you and a glorious subversive victory is the half-dozen projects and years of history you have in your existing version control tool.

Fortunately, the Subversion developers thought people might like to keep their old history around and have provided tools to convert an existing CVS[1] repository to Subversion. You can also find third-party tools to convert from ClearCase, Perforce, and Visual SourceSafe.

Before jumping headfirst into the rest of this chapter, it's worth noting that *not* converting your old repository is also a reasonable migration strategy. If you're not too bothered about being able to see historical information past the point you started using Subversion, just export your source code from the old version control tool, import it into Subversion, and make the old repository read-only. If you really do need that historical information it's still there, albeit not in the new Subversion repository.

In the rest of this chapter we'll assume you want to convert all your history and that we're performing a migration from CVS to Subversion.

---

[1] cvs2svn will also convert an RCS repository to Subversion, since RCS is the underlying format used by CVS.

B.1 Getting cvs2svn

The cvs2svn project, along with the main Subversion project, is hosted at Tigris.[2] Download the package corresponding to the version of Subversion you're using, 1.0 or 1.1.

cvs2svn is a Python script designed to run on Unix. Whilst you might be able to get it to work on Windows, possibly using the Cygwin[3] Linux emulation tools, we recommend using a real Unix box. You'll also need rcs installed because cvs2svn uses it to access the contents of your CVS repository (you can get away with having just CVS installed, but using "real" RCS is a safer bet).

You can install cvs2svn on your system so everyone can see it or just run it as a normal user. Both will work, but installing system-wide is less work if you're not Python savvy. Log in as root, and run the following commands:

```
tmp> tar -xzf cvs2svn-1.0.0.tar.gz
tmp> cd cvs2svn-1.0.0
cvs2svn-1.0.0> make install
./setup.py install
running install
    :      :      :
copying build/lib/cvs2svn_rcsparse/compat.py -> ...
copying build/lib/cvs2svn_rcsparse/debug.py -> ...
    :      :      :
byte-compiling /usr/lib/python2.3/.../default.py to default.pyc
byte-compiling /usr/lib/python2.3/.../texttools.py to texttools.pyc
running install_scripts
copying build/scripts-2.3/cvs2svn -> /usr/bin
changing mode of /usr/bin/cvs2svn to 775
```

B.2 Choosing How Much to Convert

cvs2svn will do a thorough job of converting your existing CVS repository, including all your branches and tags. It will also analyze the history, looking for files that were all changed at about the same time with the same log message and converting from CVS's per-file revision history to Subversion's changeset style. All of this is quite a bit of work and will take a while depending on the size of your CVS repository.

---

[2]http://cvs2svn.tigris.org/
[3]http://www.cygwin.com/

If you don't want to convert all of the history, you don't have to do so. Specifying which branches you're interested in will save both conversion time and space in the new Subversion repository. cvs2svn takes a whole bunch of command-line arguments, but probably the most useful is --exclude, which sets a regular expression for matching tags and branches you'd like to skip during conversion.

It's important to note that cvs2svn is designed for one-time conversions from CVS to Subversion; it can't be used to incrementally sync changes between the two systems.

B.3 Converting Your Repository

Let's assume you'd like a complete conversion of everything in your CVS repository. The first step is to make sure everyone has their changes checked into CVS and is aware you're about to do the conversion. Next take your CVS repository offline so no more changes are committed to it. The final preparation step, and the most important, is to make a copy of your CVS repository. You need to copy the whole of your CVSROOT because that's what cvs2svn runs against. We'll say that again: *make a copy of your CVS repository and use the copy when converting.*

cvs2svn works by creating a Subversion dumpfile, just like those created with svnadmin dump. The dumpfile can then be loaded into a Subversion repository with svnadmin load. You can shortcut this process using cvs2svn's -s option, specifying a directory in which you'd like to create the new Subversion repository.

Here we'll do a conversion of the Testsweet project, which is hosted on SourceForge. The great thing about SourceForge projects is the daily CVS snapshot where you can download a compressed copy of the project's repository, precisely the files cvs2svn needs for conversion.[4] If you'd like to play with cvs2svn but don't want to use your own CVS repository to do so, this might be just what you need.

---

[4]Testsweet's daily CVS snapshot is at http://cvs.sourceforge.net/cvstarballs/testsweet-cvsroot.tar.bz2.

Copy your CVS repository to a scratch directory. In this example we've put the Testsweet CVS repository into a local directory called testsweet, and we're converting it to a Subversion repository in testsweet-repos. cvs2svn will create the repository directory and initialize it for us during the conversion:

```
tmp> cvs2svn -v -s testsweet-repos testsweet
----- pass 1 -----
Examining all CVS ',v' files...
testsweet/CVSROOT/checkoutlist,v
testsweet/CVSROOT/commitinfo,v
testsweet/CVSROOT/config,v
     :      :      :
```

We asked for verboseness (the -v option), so cvs2svn produced a whole bunch of output during the conversion. Testsweet is a pretty small project so takes only a few seconds to convert. When it's done, cvs2svn prints a few statistics for us:

```
cvs2svn Statistics:
-------------------
Total CVS Files:            161
Total CVS Revisions:        218
Total Unique Tags:            1
Total Unique Branches:        0
CVS Repos Size in KB:      2716
Total SVN Commits:           10
First Revision Date:     Fri Nov 21 18:12:21 2003
Last Revision Date:      Thu Jun 24 12:35:29 2004
```

We can now use svn ls to browse the new repository, observing how we have the usual trunk, tags, and branches directories:

```
tmp> svn ls file:///tmp/testsweet-repos
branches/
tags/
trunk/
tmp> svn ls file:///tmp/testsweet-repos/trunk
CVSROOT/
testsweet/
```

We now have the Testsweet project at the root level of the repository, which might not be quite what you want. cvs2svn allows us to specify the trunk, tags, and branches directories:

```
tmp> cvs2svn --trunk=testsweet/trunk        \
             --branches=testsweet/branches  \
             --tags=testsweet/tags          \
             -s testsweet-repos testsweet
```

Your newly converted repository is ready for use immediately. Just fire up networking using svnserve or Apache, check out a working copy, and carry on coding!

Third-Party Subversion Tools

Subversion comes as a set of command-line applications—svn, svnadmin, svnserve, etc. Whilst the command line is fairly easy to use, most people like to use something a little more friendly. Fortunately, Subversion provides a rich set of APIs to third-party developers, so they can make add-on clients and tools.

C.1 TortoiseSVN

Tortoise is a front end for Subversion that integrates directly with Windows Explorer. Once installed, you can see the state of your files and directories just by browsing around your computer. Tortoise puts little green ticks next to files that are up-to-date and little red exclamation points next to files you've modified. Tortoise also provides handy automation for tasks such as resolving conflicts and managing tags and branches.

In this section we'll use Tortoise to carry out some everyday tasks that we've previously seen using the command line.

Downloading and Installing

Download TortoiseSVN,[1] and run the appropriate installer for your version of Windows, which should pop up a welcome screen. Pick a location to install to (or accept the default directory C:\Program Files\TortoiseSVN), and choose whether Tortoise should be available to every user on the computer or just

---

[1]TortoiseSVN can be found at http://tortoisesvn.tigris.org/.

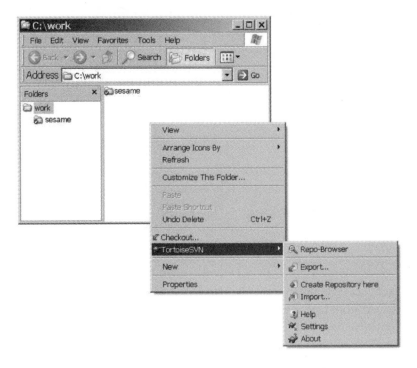

Figure C.1: THE TORTOISE CONTEXT MENU

yourself. That's all you need to decide on; the installer will take care of everything else.

The Tortoise installer will ask you to restart your computer. Unlike most installers Tortoise is actually serious about this; because it integrates with the Windows Explorer, it needs a reboot to properly register itself.

Checking Out

Bring up an Explorer window, and change to a directory in which you'd like to check out a working copy. Here we'll be using C:\work. Right-clicking in the directory will bring up a menu including Tortoise's Subversion integration, as shown in Figure C.1.

Choose *Checkout...* from the context menu, which will bring up a dialog box asking what you'd like to check out. Use the sandbox repository file:///C:/svn-repos/sesame/trunk, and check

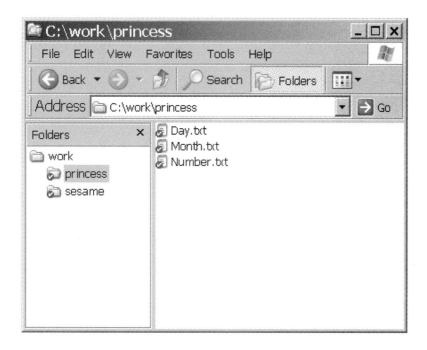

Figure C.2: THE FRESHLY CHECKED-OUT SESAME PROJECT

out to C:\work\princess (sesame is already a working copy, so we'll be starting fresh as Princess).

Tortoise will flash a progress box as it checks out the Sesame project, leaving you with a new princess directory. Looking in the directory, you'll see Day.txt, Number.txt, and the rest of the Sesame project. Since all the files are up-to-date, Tortoise flags them with a little green check mark, as shown in Figure C.2.

Making Changes

Make some changes to Number.txt, maybe capitalizing *three*. After you save the file, Tortoise will flag it with a red exclamation point.[2] The parent directory princess will also be flagged red. Right-click Number.txt, and choose *TortoiseSVN > Diff.*

---

[2]You might need to hit F5 to get Windows to refresh the screen and display the new icon.

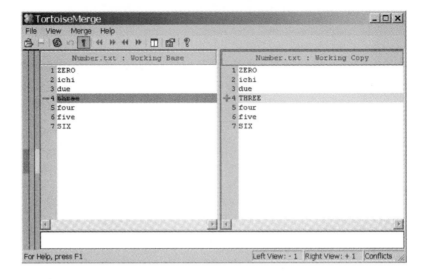

Figure C.3: Examining Your Changes

This will display a TortoiseMerge window showing the changes you've made, similar to Figure C.3.

Adding a new file is equally straightforward. Create a new file called Year.txt, and save it in your working copy. Subversion doesn't know anything about this file yet, so Tortoise leaves it undecorated. Right-click the new file, and choose *Tortoise-eSVN > Add*. Tortoise will pop up a window asking you to confirm the addition, which is more useful when you're adding a bunch of files at once. Click the OK button, and Tortoise will add the file. Since Subversion now knows about Year.txt, it displays it with a blue "plus" icon.

Checking In

Right-click on the princess directory, and choose *Commit....* Tortoise will show you all the files you've changed and prompt you for a commit message, as shown in Figure C.4 on the next page. At this point, you can decide not to commit a particular file by unchecking its tickbox. If you're not sure what you've changed, double-clicking a file will pop up a diff window so you can review your changes.

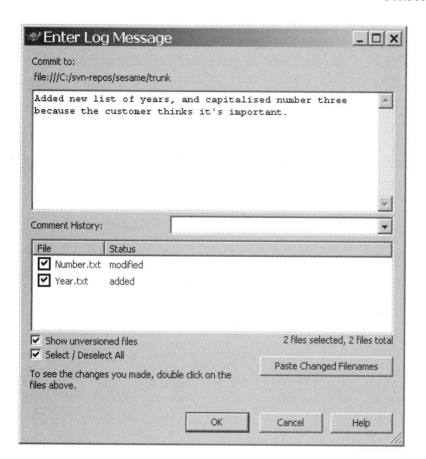

Figure C.4: THE TORTOISESVN COMMIT WINDOW

Enter a commit message describing your changes (and more important *why* you made those changes) and hit OK. Tortoise will flash a window as it commits your changes to the repository.

Resolving Conflicts

As part of our lightning-fast tour through Tortoise, let's see how it helps us when a conflict arises. Check out another copy of the Sesame project, this time to C:\work\aladdin. We'll use this directory to simulate the actions of Aladdin, another developer on our team. Edit Number.txt, changing *five* to *cinco*, and then commit the changes.

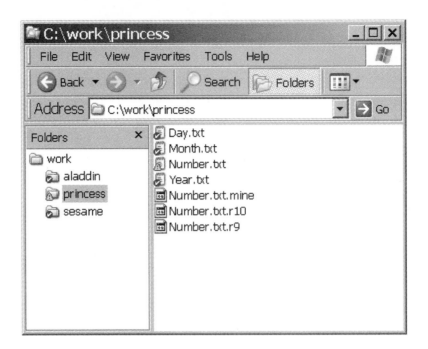

Figure C.5: NUMBER.TXT IN CONFLICT

Now go back to the princess working copy, and edit the same file, changing *five* to *cinq*, this time to keep our French customers happy. Right-click the princess directory, choose *Commit*, enter a log message, and hit OK. Tortoise will tell you that Number.txt is out-of-date and the commit has failed. Tortoise will also suggest you update your working copy in order to commit.

Follow Tortoise's suggestion, and run an update on princess by right-clicking and choosing *Update*. The Tortoise update window will pop up whilst Tortoise gets the latest revision from the repository, and depending on how fast your machine is you might notice a line in red as it gets to Number.txt, denoting a conflict. Tortoise will leave both Number.txt and princess decorated with a warning triangle, as shown in Figure C.5, to let you know there's a conflict.

Tortoise also saves some extra copies of Number.txt to help resolve the conflict. You'll notice .mine, .r9, and .r10 in our

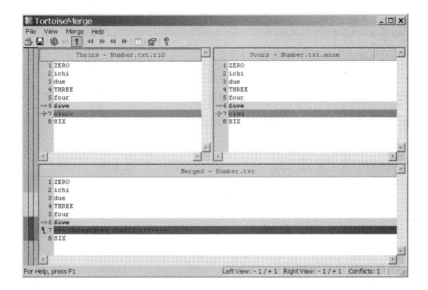

Figure C.6: THE TORTOISE MERGE WINDOW

example so far. The first, .mine, is your version of the file, including your modifications. The second, .r9, contains the base revision on which your changes are based—this is the revision of the file before Princess started editing it. Finally, .r10 contains the revision that conflicts with your changes. These are the changes that Aladdin committed.

Fortunately, Tortoise comes with a three-way[3] merge tool that makes it easy to resolve the conflicts. Right-click on the file Number.txt, and choose *TortoiseSVN > Edit Conflicts*. Tortoise will pop up a merge window like that in Figure C.6.

TortoiseMerge displays the two sets of changes side by side, along with a merge result in the bottom half of the window. In this particular case we're sure that *cinq* is correct, so we're going to pick our changes (the Princess's changes rather than Aladdin's). Right-click the word *cinq*, and choose *Use this text block*. Tortoise will update the merge result in the bottom half of the window to show the result. If you have more than

---

[3]Three-way merging is so called because it merges an original version of a file with two people's changes.

one conflict, you can pick and choose between the two sets of changes until you're happy. Now just close the merge window. Tortoise will ask you if you'd like to save your changes; say "yes" since you're happy with the merge, and Tortoise will close the merge window.

You'll notice Tortoise is still decorating the file with a little warning triangle. Now that we've resolved the conflict, we need to tell Tortoise everything is okay. Right-click Number.txt, and choose *TortoiseSVN > Resolved*. Tortoise will clean up the .mine, .r9, and .r10 files and mark Number.txt with an exclamation point showing you've modified it. Now finish checking in as normal.

TortoiseSVN provides shortcuts for branching, tagging, and merging, and whilst we don't have space here to detail everything, we do suggest you try it. We do just about have room to plug the excellent repository browser, which you can get to by choosing *TortoiseSVN > Repo-Browser*. This nifty little tool enables you to nose around a repository without needing a working copy. This comes in handy if you're trying to figure out where all the branches are for a project or where exactly they've imported vendor source code. Figure C.7 on the facing page shows us perusing the Subversion repository at http://svn.collab.net.

C.2 IDE Integration

Subversion's IDE integration is in its early stages but is gathering momentum almost daily. It's possible to use just the command line or Tortoise, but many users are used to tight integration between their editor and version control, so there are many projects working on Subversion integration.

Eclipse, the popular open-source Java IDE, has a plug-in called Subclipse that integrates with Subversion, available from http://subclipse.tigris.org/.

IntelliJ IDEA, another popular Java IDE, has full "official" support for Subversion planned in release 5. You'll find an early access program (EAP) build at http://intellij.net/ eap/. If you don't want to use the EAP version or to wait for IDEA 5, there are a number of open-source plug-ins available.

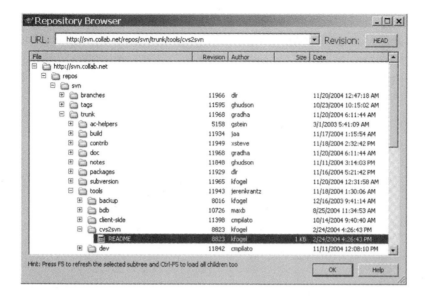

Figure C.7: TORTOISE REPO-BROWSER IN ACTION

Two of the most popular are `http://svnup.tigris.org/` and `http://svn4eclipse.tigris.org/`.

Ankhsvn provides integration with Visual Studio and is available from `http://ankhsvn.tigris.org/`. Note that if you're using Visual Studio web projects, they may be incompatible with Subversion's .svn administrative directories. You can download a special build of TortoiseSVN that uses _svn to work around this problem—make sure you pick the right version when downloading!

C.3 Other Tools

SVN::Notify sends colored HTML e-mails when a developer checks changes into your repository. This can be a great communication tool for your team. SVN::Notify is available from CPAN: `http://search.cpan.org/dist/SVN-Notify/`.

If you're using XCode on the Mac, you might need a key manager to get SSH connections to work. SSHKeychain provides "painless key management for Mac OS X" and is available from `http://www.sshkeychain.org/`.

The Putty suite of SSH client tools for Windows[4] also works great for getting an svn+ssh connection working and includes Pageant, a key management agent. Chapters 8 and 9 of the Putty Manual[5] are worth reading if you'd like to avoid typing passwords everytime you access an svn+ssh repository.

---

[4]http://www.chiark.greenend.org.uk/~sgtatham/putty/
[5]http://the.earth.li/~sgtatham/putty/0.56/htmldoc/Chapter9.html

Command Summary and Recipes

D.1 Subversion Command Summary

Most Subversion commands have common options, which we list first in order to avoid repeating them for each command. If you're unsure what options a particular command accepts, just run svn help *command* for a quick summary.

Common options:

--targets	*list*	Read in *list* and interpret it as a list of arguments on which to operate.
--non-recursive, -N		Operate on a single directory only; don't try to process subdirectories.
--verbose, -v		Print additional information.
--quiet, -q		Print as little as possible.
--username	*name*	Specify the name to be used when connecting and authorizing.
--password	*pswd*	Specify the password to be used.
--no-auth-cache		Do not cache authentication tokens.
--non-interactive		Do not prompt for extra information.
--config-dir	*dir*	Read user configuration from *dir*.
--editor-cmd	*cmd*	Use *cmd* as log message editor.

svn add

Add names of files and directories to version control. They will be added to the repository in the next commit.

```
svn add path...
```

Options:

--autoprops	Automatically set properties on files when adding them.
--no-autoprops	Disable automatic property setting.

svn blame   (also known as ann, annotate, praise)

Show revision and author information for each line of a file

```
svn blame target...
```

Options:

--revision, -r   *rev*   If specified as a single revision *rev*, show blame information for the targets at revision *rev*. If specified as a revision range *rev1:rev2*, show blame information for the targets at revision *rev2*, but examine revisions only as far back as *rev1* (for this to be useful, *rev1* should be less than *rev2*).

svn cat

Output the contents of specified files or URLs.

```
svn cat target...
```

Options:

--revision, –r   *rev*   Output the contents of *target* at revision *rev*.

svn checkout   (also known as co)

Check out a working copy from a repository.

```
svn checkout url... path
```

Checks out the given URLs. With no path argument, checks out into local directories named using the base names of the URLs. If path is given with one URL argument, checks out into path. If path is given with multiple URL arguments, checks out into subdirectories of path named for the base names in the urls.

Options:

--revision, -r   *rev*   The revision to check out.

svn cleanup

Clean up the working copy, removing locks, resuming unfinished operations, etc.

```
svn cleanup path...
```

svn commit   (also known as ci)

Send changes from your working copy to the repository.

```
svn commit path...
```

Options:

--message, –m	msg	Use msg as the commit log message.
--file, –F	file	Use the contents of file as the commit log message.

svn copy

Duplicate something in working copy or repository, remembering history.

```
svn copy src dest
```

src and dest can each be either a working copy (WC) path or a URL.

src	dest	Effect...
WC	WC	Copy and schedule for addition (with history).
WC	URL	Immediately commit a copy of WC to URL.
URL	WC	Check out URL into WC, schedule for addition.
URL	URL	Complete server-side copy; used to branch and tag.

Options:

--revision, -r	rev	The revision of src to copy. Only makes sense if src is a repository URL.

svn delete   (also known as del, remove, rm)

Remove files and directories from version control.

```
svn delete target...
```

Deletes files and directories from the repository. If target is a working copy file or directory, it is removed from the working copy and scheduled for deletion at the next commit. If target is a repository URL, it is deleted from the repository via an immediate commit.

Options:

--message, –m	msg	Use msg as the commit log message.
--file, –F	file	Use the contents of file as the commit log message.

svn diff

Display the differences between two paths.

```
svn diff -rrev1:rev2 target...
svn diff oldurl newurl
```

In the first form, display changes made to *target* between revisions *rev1* and *rev2*. Targets may be working copy paths or URLs.

In the second form, display the differences between the HEAD revisions of *oldurl* and *newurl*.

Options:

--old	*arg*	Use *arg* as the older target.
--new	*arg*	Use *arg* as the newer target.

svn export

Create an unversioned copy of a tree.

```
svn export -rrev URL path
```

Exports a clean directory tree from the repository specified by *URL*, at revision *rev* if it is given, otherwise at HEAD, into *path*. If *path* is omitted the last component of the URL is used as the local directory name.

Options:

--revision, -r	*rev*	Export from the repository at revision *rev*.
--native-eol	*style*	Use a different end-of-line marker than the standard system marker for files with a native svn:eol-style property. *style* must be one of LF, CR, or CRLF.

svn import

Commit an unversioned file or tree into the repository.

```
svn import path URL
```

Recursively commit a copy of *path* to *URL*. If *path* is omitted, the current directory is assumed. Parent directories are created as necessary in the repository.

Options:

--autoprops	Automatically set properties on files when importing them.
--no-autoprops	Disable automatic property setting on imported files.

svn info

Display information about a file or directory.

```
svn info path...
```

Print information about each *path.*

Options:

--recursive, -r   Descend recursively.

svn list   (also known as ls)

List directory entries in the repository.

```
svn list target...
```

List each *target* file and the contents of each *target* directory as they exist in the repository. If *target* is a working copy path, the corresponding repository URL will be used.

Options:

--verbose, -v   Show extra information about each directory entry.

svn log

Show the log messages for a set of revisions and/or files.

```
svn log target
```

Print the log messages for a local path or repository URL. For a local path the default revision range is BASE:1, and for a URL the default revision range is HEAD:1.

Options:

--revision, -r   *rev*   If *rev* is a single revision, show the log entry only for that revision. If *rev* is a revision range, show only the log entries for those revisions.

--verbose, -v   Print all affected paths with each log message.

--stop-on-copy   Do not cross copies while traversing history (useful for determining the start point of a branch).

svn merge

Apply the differences between two sources to a working copy path.

```
svn merge sourceURL1@rev1 sourceURL2@rev2 wcpath
svn merge sourceWCPATH1@rev1 sourceWCPATH2@rev1 wcpath
svn merge -r rev1:rev2 SOURCE wcpath
```

In the first form, the source URLs are specified at revisions *rev1* and *rev2*. These are the two sources to be compared. The revisions default to HEAD if omitted.

In the second form, the URLs corresponding to the source working copy paths define the sources to be compared. The revisions must be specified.

In the third form, SOURCE can be a URL or working copy item, in which case the corresponding URL is used. This URL is compared as it existed between revisions *rev1* and *rev2*.

wcpath is the working copy path that will receive the changes. If *wcpath* is omitted, a the current directory is assumed, unless the sources have identical basenames that match a file within the current directory, in which case the differences will be applied to that file.

Options:

--diff3-cmd	*cmd*	Use *cmd* as merge command.
--ignore-ancestry		Ignore ancestry when calculating merges.

svn mkdir

Create a new directory under version control.

```
svn mkdir target...
```

Each directory specified by a working copy path is created locally and scheduled for addition upon the next commit. Each directory specified by a URL is created in the repository via an immediate commit.

In both cases, all the intermediate directories must already exist.

svn move   (also known as mv, rename, ren)

Move and/or rename something in working copy or repository.

```
svn move src dest
```

src and *dest* must both be either working copy paths or repository URLs. In the working copy, the move is performed and the new location scheduled for addition. For repository URLs, a complete server-side rename is performed immediately.

Options:

--revision, -r   *rev*   Use revision *rev* of the source when performing the move.

svn propdel   (also known as pdel, pd)

Remove property from files or directories.

```
svn propdel propname path...
```

Delete property *propname* from *path* in the local working copy.

svn propedit   (also known as pedit, pe)

Edit property on files or directories.

```
svn propedit propname path...
```

Start an external editor, and edit *propname* on *path* in the local working copy.

svn propget   (also known as pget, pg)

Print property values from files or directories.

```
svn propget propname path...
```

Print the contents of *propname* from each *path.* By default, Subversion will add an extra newline to the end of the property values so that the output looks pretty. Also, whenever there are multiple paths involved, each property value is prefixed with the path with which it is associated.

Options:

--strict   Disable extra newlines and other beautifications (useful when redirecting binary property values to a file).

svn proplist   (also known as plist, pl)

List all properties on files or directories.

```
svn proplist path...
```

List properties on *path*.

Options:

--verbose, -v		Print extra information.
--recursive, -R		Descend recursively.
--revision, -r	*rev*	List properties defined in revision *rev* of *path*.

svn propset   (also known as pset, ps)

Set a propery on files or directories.

```
svn propset propname propval path...
```

Set property *propname* to value *propval* on *path*. If *propval* is not specified, you must use the -F option to specify a file whose contents should be used as the property value.

Options:

--file, -F	*file*	Read the contents of *file* and use it as the property value.
--recursive, -R		Descend recursively.
--encoding	*enc*	Treat value as being in character set encoding *enc*.

svn resolved

Remove conflicted state on working copy files or directories.

```
svn resolved path...
```

Mark a file that previously contained conflicts as "resolved." Note that this command does not semantically resolve conflicts or remove conflict markers; it merely removes the conflict-related artifact files and allows *path* to be committed.

Options:

--recursive, -R	Descend recursively.

svn revert

Restore pristine working copy file (undo most local edits).

```
svn revert path...
```

This command does not require network access and undoes any changes you have made to *path*. It does not restore removed directories.

Options:

--recursive, -R   Descend recursively.

svn status   (also known as stat, st)

Print the status of working copy files and directories.

```
svn status path...
```

With no args, print only locally modified items (no network access). With -u, add working revision and server out-of-date information. With -v, print full revision information on every item.

The first five columns in the output are each one character wide.

First column: Says if item was added, deleted, or otherwise changed.

" "   No modifications.
A   Added.
C   Conflicted.
D   Deleted.
G   Merged.
I   Ignored.
M   Modified.
R   Replaced.
X   Item is unversioned, but is used by an externals definition.
?   Item is not under version control.
!   Item is missing (removed by non-svn command) or incomplete.
~   Versioned item obstructed by some item of a different kind.

Second column: Modifications of a file's or directory's properties.

" "   No modifications.
C   Conflicted.
M   Modified.

Third column: Whether the working copy directory is locked.

" "   Not locked.
L   Locked.

Fourth column: Scheduled commit will contain addition with history.

" "   No history scheduled with commit.
+   History scheduled with commit.

Fifth column: Whether the item is switched relative to its parent.

" "   Normal.
S   Switched.

The out-of-date information appears in the eighth column (with -u).

*   A newer revision exists on the server.
" "   The working copy is up-to-date.

The remaining fields are variable width and delimited by spaces: the working revision (with -u or -v), the last-committed revision, and last-committed author (with -v). The working copy path is always the final field, so it can include spaces.

Options:

--show-updates, -u	Contact the server to display update information.
--verbose, -v	Print extra information.
--non-recursive, -N	Operate on single directory only.
--no-ignore	Disregard default and svn:ignore property ignores.

svn switch   (also known as sw)

Update the working copy to a different URL.

```
svn switch URL path
```

Update the working copy to mirror a new URL within the repository. This behavior is similar to svn update and is the way to move a working copy to a branch or tag within the same repository.

Options:

--revision, -r	rev	Switch to revision rev.
--non-recursive, -N		Operate on single directory only.
--diff3-cmd	cmd	Use cmd as merge command.

svn update   (also known as up)

Bring changes from the repository into the working copy.

```
svn update path...
```

If no revision given, bring working copy up-to-date with HEAD revision. Otherwise synchronize working copy to revision given by -r.

For each updated item a line will start with a character reporting the action taken. These characters have the following meaning:

A   Added.
D   Deleted.
U   Updated.
C   Conflict.
M   Merged.

A character in the first column signifies an update to the actual file, and updates to the file's properties are shown in the second column.

Options:

--revision, -r	*rev*	Update to revision *rev*.
--non-recursive, -N		Operate on single directory only.
--diff3-cmd	*cmd*	Use *cmd* as merge command.

D.2 Recipes

Setting a property on a file or directory .... *Page 68*
> svn propset *propname propvalue path*...

Editing a property on a file or directory .... *Page 68*
> svn propedit *propname path*...

Listing the properties on a file or directory .... *Page 68*
> svn proplist *path*...

Printing the contents of a property .... *Page 68*
> svn propget *propname path*...

Deleting a property .... *Page 69*
> svn propdel *propname path*...

Enabling keyword expansion for a file .... *Page 70*
> svn propset svn:keywords "*keywords*" *file*...

Ignoring certain files in a directory .... *Page 72*
> svn propedit svn:ignore *path*...

Setting end-of-line style for a file .... *Page 73*
> svn propset svn:eol-style *style path*...

Setting the mime-type of file .... *Page 74*
> svn propset svn:mime-type *mime-type path*...

Marking a file executable .... *Page 75*
> svn propset svn:executable true *path*...

Copying a file or directory .... *Page 77*
> svn copy *source destination*

Renaming a file or directory .... *Page 78*
> svn rename *oldname newname*

Moving a file or directory .... *Page 78*
> svn move *source destination*

Showing changes to a file or directory .... *Page 81*
> svn diff *path*...

Comparing two revisions of a file .... *Page 82*
> svn diff -r*rev1*:*rev2 file*

Showing changes between a file and the latest revision in the repository .... *Page 84*
> svn diff -r HEAD *file*...

```
cd work

svn checkout    \

   svn://myserver/project/branches/RB-x.y
```

```
cd myproj

svn switch    \

   svn://myserver/project/branches/RB-x.y
```

```
cd myproj

svn switch svn://myserver/project/trunk
```

```
svn copy    \

   svn://myserver/project/branches/RB-x.y    \

   svn://myserver/project/tags/REL-x.y
```

```
svn checkout    \

   svn://myserver/project/tags/REL-x.y
```

```
cd project

svn update

svn merge -rrev-1:rev    \

   svn://myserver/project/branches/RB-x.y
```

```
svn copy    \

   svn://myserver/project/branches/RB-x.y    \

   svn://myserver/project/branches/BUG-track

svn copy    \

   svn://myserver/project/branches/BUG-track \

   svn://myserver/project/tags/PRE-track
```

```
svn checkout    \

   svn://myserver/project/branches/BUG-track
```

```
svn copy    \

   svn://myserver/project/branches/BUG-track \

   svn://myserver/project/tags/POST-track
```

Merging a complex bug fix to a release branch .... *Page 118*
```
cd RBx.y

svn merge    \
  svn://myserver/project/tags/PRE-track    \
  svn://myserver/project/tags/POST-track
```

Creating experimental branches .... *Page 119*
```
svn copy    \
  svn://.../trunk    \
  svn://.../branches/TRY-initials-mnemonic
```

Using an experimental branch .... *Page 119*
```
svn switch    \
  svn://.../branches/TRY-initials-mnemonic
```

Returning to the trunk .... *Page 119*
```
svn switch svn://.../trunk
```

Finding out when a branch was created .... *Page 120*
```
svn log --stop-on-copy    \
        svn://.../branches/branch
```

Merging an experimental branch .... *Page 121*
```
svn log --stop-on-copy    \
  svn://.../branches/TRY-initials-mnemonic
cd trunk-working-copy
svn merge    \
  -r branch-start-revision:HEAD    \
  svn://.../branches/TRY-initials-mnemonic
svn commit
```

Importing a project into the repository .... *Page 125*
```
cd project
svn import svn://myserver/project/trunk
```

Manually creating directories for a project .... *Page 125*
```
svn mkdir svn://myserver/project/
svn mkdir svn://myserver/project/trunk
svn mkdir svn://myserver/project/tags
svn mkdir svn://myserver/project/branches
```

Importing third-party code .... *Page 141*
```
svn import vendor-tree    \
  svn://.../vendorsrc/vendor/product/current
```

Tagging a vendor drop . . . . *Page 142*
```
svn copy     \
  svn://.../vendorsrc/vendor/product/current \
  svn://.../vendorsrc/vendor/product/version
```

Loading a new vendor drop . . . . *Page 143*
```
svn_load_dirs.pl     \
    svn://.../vendorsrc/vendor/product    \
    current vendor-tree
```

Using vendor code in a project . . . . *Page 144*
```
svn copy     \
  svn://.../vendorsrc/vendor/product/ver \
  svn://.../project/trunk/vendor/product
```

Upgrading vendor code in a project . . . . *Page 145*
```
svn merge    \
  svn://.../vendorsrc/vendor/product/oldver \
  svn://.../vendorsrc/vendor/product/newver \
  vendor/product
```

Starting svnserve on Windows . . . . *Page 148*
```
start svnserve --daemon --root repos-dir
```

Starting svnserve on Unix . . . . *Page 149*
```
svnserve --daemon --root repos-dir
```

Creating a full backup of your repository . . . . *Page 164*
```
svnadmin dump repos > dumpfile
```

Creating an incremental backup of your repository . *Page 165*
```
svnadmin dump --incremental    \
    --revision rev1:rev2 repos
```

Appendix E

Other Resources

There are a wealth of Subversion and verson control related resources available out there—here are just a few to get you started.

E.1 Online Resources

Subversion Home Page .... `http://subversion.tigris.org/`
The official Subversion web site is an excellent resource for anyone getting started with Subversion. The site contains all sorts of documentation, including the excellent Subversion FAQ that contains common questions and answers. The project links page is a great place to find Subversion-related software, plug-ins, articles, and documentation.

You can also join the Subversion users' mailing list; just send an e-mail to `users-subscribe@subversion.tigris.org`. The list is *the* place to ask questions and is populated by some very friendly people, including Subversion's core developers.

Pragmatic Programmers. . .
. . . `http://www.pragmaticprogrammer.com/titles/svn/`
The companion web site for this book where you'll find code samples, errata, and links to other pragmatic things.

Subversion Book............`http://svnbook.red-bean.com/`
The official Subversion book is available online and in print form and contains in-depth discussion of even Subversion's most esoteric features.

Better SCM................`http://better-scm.berlios.de/`
The Better SCM project aims to promote alternatives to CVS and includes a comparison between various version control systems.

CM Crossroads . . . . http://www.cmcrossroads.com/
Configuration Management is a larger topic than version control but usually requires decent version control to achieve its aims. If you're interested in how source code, builds, projects, and releases are organized, this site contains articles and discussion groups that may interest you.

E.2 Bibliography

[BA03]   Stephen P. Berczuk and Brad Appleton. *Soft-ware Configuration Management Patterns: Effec-tive Teamwork, Practical Integration.* Addison-Wes-ley, 2003.

[Cla04]   Mike Clark. *Pragmatic Project Automation. How to Build, Deploy, and Monitor Java Applications.* The Pragmatic Programmers, LLC, Raleigh, NC, and Dallas, TX, 2004.

[HT03]   Andrew Hunt and David Thomas. *Pragmatic Unit Testing In Java with JUnit.* The Pragmatic Pro-grammers, LLC, Raleigh, NC, and Dallas, TX, 2003.

Index

T

U